THE VIEW FROM THE OTHER SIDE OF MY HEAD

THE VIEW FROM THE OTHER SIDE OF MY HEAD

Seth Steinzor

GREEN PLACE BOOKS
Brattleboro, Vermont

Printed in the United States

10 9 8 7 6 5 4 3 2 1

Green Writers Press is a Vermont-based publisher whose mission is to spread a message of hope and renewal through the words and images we publish. Throughout we will adhere to our commitment to preserving and protecting the natural resources of the earth. To that end, a percentage of our proceeds will be donated to environmental and social-activist groups. Green Writers Press gratefully acknowledges support from individual donors, friends, and readers to help support the environment and our publishing initiative. Green Place Books curates books that tell literary and compelling stories with a focus on writing about place—these books are more personal stories/memoir and biographies.

GREEN PLACE BOOKS Green writers press

Giving Voice to Writers & Artists Who Will Make the World a Better Place
Green Writers Press | Brattleboro, Vermont
www.greenwriterspress.com

ISBN: 979-8-9914134-0-4

COVER ART ISTOCKPHOTO_STEREOHYPE

MIX
Paper | Supporting responsible forestry
FSC® C103525
FSC www.fsc.org

PRINTED AT KASE PRINTERS, ON FSC-CERTIFIED PAPER AND PRINTED WITH SOY-BASED INK, DEDICATED TO SOUND ENVIRONMENTAL PRACTICES AND MAKING ONGOING EFFORTS TO REDUCE OUR CARBON FOOTPRINT. WITH PAPER AS A CORE PART OF OUR BUSINESS, KASE IS COMMITTED TO IMPLEMENTING POLICIES THAT FACILITATE CONSERVATION AND SUSTAINABLE PRACTICES. KASE SOURCES PRINTING PAPERS FROM RESPONSIBLE MILLS AND DISTRIBUTORS THAT ARE CERTIFIED WITH AT LEAST ONE CERTIFICATION FROM AN INDEPENDENT THIRD PARTY VERIFICATION, SOURCED DIRECTLY FROM RESPONSIBLY MANAGED FORESTS. WE ALSO MAKE ONGOING EFFORTS TO REDUCE OUR CARBON FOOTPRINT, REUSE ENERGY AND RESOURCES, MINIMIZE WASTE DURING THE MANUFACTURING PROCESS, AND RECYCLE 100% OF SCRAPS, TRASH, CARTRIDGES, EQUIPMENT, AND SOLVENTS WHENEVER POSSIBLE. WE ARE A FAMILY-RUN BUSINESS, LOCATED IN HUDSON, NEW HAMPSHIRE.

". . . how very great and complex this world is, so much so that one cannot possibly comprehend it in thought—no doubt only in fragments, the bits and pieces of small understandings."

—Elzbieta Druzbacka, poet, a character in Olga Tokarczuk's novel *The Books of Jacob*, trans. Jennifer Croft (Riverhead Books 2022), p. 887

"Although I would very much like to, I am unable to make a record of everything, for after all, things are so inextricably bound together that should I merely tap the tip of my pen against one, then it nudges another, and soon a great sea has unfurled itself before me. What kind of dam are the edges of my paper, is the trail of ink I leave? How, then, would I be able to express all that my soul has received in this life, and in a single book, at that?"

—Rabbi Nahman of Busk, in *The Books of Jacob*, p. 740

THE VIEW FROM THE OTHER SIDE OF MY HEAD

INTRODUCTION

This book chronicles my early education in shamanic trance. To its subject it owes several peculiarities of form, style, and substance. My aim has been to describe the process of stumbling into the dreamworld as faithfully as I can to the actual experience of doing so, with sufficient clarity so as not to bewilder the reader, sufficient honesty so that the reader can feel my own bewilderment, and sufficient comprehensiveness so that the reader can discern how thoroughly my world was reconfigured.

In writing this book, I've been particularly mindful of those readers who may be interested in embarking upon their own set of Journeys. For their sake, I've endeavored to present a raw, unvarnished view of my forays into the dreamworld. To go there is such a solitary venture, often a lonely one (to whom can you talk about this stuff?), nearly always deeply disorienting. Our culture provides next to no support for this, outside a growing body of niche literature of mostly dubious helpfulness, and little clear guidance. To happen upon good teachers, as I did, is a matter of luck, not something that one can count on. I hope that people becoming newly acquainted with the dreamworld will find in my book a bit of the sustenance of community and shared experience.

In keeping with that ambition, this is neither a treatise on shamanism nor a "how-to-be-a-shaman" guidebook. There are plenty of those. This is about what it was like for an American in his late sixties, a lawyer by training and profession, an agnostic Jew, to crash through the looking glass into Wonderland and then to find his feet there.

This book is addressed primarily to inheritors of cultures that long ago lost or abandoned their own shamanic practices and traditions. So far as I am aware, the history of those tragic losses has yet to be written. In *Religion and the Decline of Magic* (Penguin University Books 1973), Keith Thomas made the case that widespread English folk belief in magical healing, defined in such a way as to possibly include English forms of shamanism, succumbed in the sixteenth and seventeenth centuries to changing material conditions and competition from Protestant religion, and later, science. May one generalize from the English experience? Perhaps; but it is a large, multifarious world, and the decline of shamanism is a global phenomenon. Be that as it may, those with no direct access to trance and the dreamworld must look to cultures other than their own, if they wish to restore that connection. Many Indigenous societies have resisted acculturation successfully enough to retain a living link, in the persons of shamans. To them, those of us lacking such traditions must look for guidance.

Yanomamo shaman Davi Kopenawa refers to white Brazilians and the other representatives of the non-Indigenous West whom he has encountered with the epithet "the People of Merchandise." Nothing in America escapes monetization, the dollar being chief among the values the dominant society respects. Now that interest in shamanic practice is enjoying a tentative revival, possibly in reaction to the spiritual starvation of advanced capitalism, there's an accompanying market for what Stephen Colbert might call "shamaniness."

One of the first books I consulted, at the beginning of my Journeying, when I was struggling for something solid to hold onto like a child thrown into the deep end of the pool, has a cover that perfectly illustrates what I mean. It features an attractive youngish person of indeterminate gender wearing a sort of Navajo blanket robe, a beaded necklace with a bear pendant, a dream catcher earring, and a headdress made of a giant eagle head and turkey feathers. This vaguely non-white person brandishes a deer antler, gazing sternly off to the side, where an elk stands beneath a couple of raptors that fly in front of a big, orange sun. The book purports to tell us about the symbolic meanings of animals.

The book's cover is a perfect example of cultural appropriation. For purposes of self-interest not compelled by survival, that is, to sell books, it invokes stereotypical images of cultures other than the one of which it is a part, in order to draw over itself a mantle of spurious knowledge, authority, and authenticity relating to them. I say "stereotypical," because that is the crime at the heart of cultural appropriation: a denial or minimization of others' humanity, a commodification of people. I stress "self-interest" because cultural appropriation occurs not only in the service of pecuniary advantage, but for other reasons as well, for example, to establish a personal identity in a group without that group's full knowledge of or consent to the circumstances. I add the caveat "not compelled by survival" because often in human history members of economically, militarily, politically, and socially disadvantaged groups have found it necessary to adopt characteristics of the dominant group in order to be allowed to live.

Cultural appropriation is a lion in the path of anyone in our culture who wants to explore the dreamworld. It is unavoidable and it must be confronted. A person who comes from a culture having no language or systematic body of ideas about the dreamworld, has no choice but to borrow language and ideas from other cultures, or that person cannot talk about it at all. But honesty, anti-racism, and decent humility demand transparency about the provenance of such borrowings, precision in usage of them, respect for their cultural contexts, and full acknowledgement of the borrowers' overwhelming ignorance.

In this book, I use a vocabulary and conceptual framework borrowed from Polynesian shamanic traditions because that is the culture from which my teachers derived their knowledge of trance and the dreamworld. But neither they nor I pretend to possess expertise regarding Polynesian shamanism. On the other hand, if you want to know what it was like to stumble into the dreamworld largely unprepared, I am happy to oblige you.

It has been a long trail already. Everything on the path was unpremeditated, unexpected. Because this is the journal of an education, it is full of seeming failures and false starts. The plot, such as it is, does not proceed with anything like the straightness of an arrow. It meanders and twists back on itself, takes strange leaps. The continuity between events is not always apparent until they are over.

The dreamworld, as its appellation suggests, is a place of mutability and otherness. But it also is a place that I enter as a conscious agent, a person identifiably myself if somewhat altered in certain characteristics. For example, in the dreamworld I'm not very articulate. I witness events there, and take active part in them. Among my earliest and strongest impressions of trance was that the objects, entities, and personalities I meet there exist autonomously of my will. I feel, with a certainty equivalent to that with which I lower myself to a chair in full confidence that it will support my weight when I sit on it, that I am encountering a "real" world, in fact the world I am used to, but perceived through a vastly different set of lenses from those to which I'm accustomed. I don't control the dreamworld, for the most part. I am there as a witness to whatever it presents me with, following events that occur according to a logic or set of logics very alien to that which apply in ordinary consciousness. (For example, you normally can't walk up stairs and down them at the same time.) Perforce, this book, a record of such encounters, is shaped by them.

The Journeys recounted herein took me through my own, almost forgotten history of childhood trauma; to encounters with the overwhelming power of a presence beyond human individuality, beyond words, to which I am connected, whose roots are in my body; to a renewed acquaintance with and respect for my ancestors; to conversations with a tree and a rock; to a rite of dismemberment and reconstitution. All this in the kindergarten phase of my education! But it's important to stay grounded. What I experience in trance has profound impacts on everyday life. The same is true, vice versa. That intercourse between the quotidian and the dreamworld is the thread that runs through this book, holding it together.

It's not just a question of juxtaposing what I viewed in the dreamworld's seemingly distorted funhouse mirror against the hard-edged, clear, windowpane vision that we like to think represents our whole experience of daily life. Both perspectives on reality reach far beyond such simple oppositions, which, presented in the language of ordinary consciousness, inevitably skew invidiously against what sounds like the strangeness of trance. But shamanic consciousness is as inherent to us as the one we think we live by. In a somewhat desperate effort to find my balance by identifying the plane on which both these modes of consciousness coincide, I developed a fascination with the neurology of trance. It is a newly developing and as yet much understudied field of investigation. A small but important section of this book concerns my research into biological epistemology, what I learned from it, and the questions it raised.

One of the entities I often encounter in trance goes by the name of Fox. Sometimes he has the appearance of a red fox. Sometimes he looks like a filament of scarlet flame, or a tangle of them. Fox, who is always happy to offer advice, says that the book should include these lines by T.S. Eliot:

We shall not cease from exploration
And the end of all our exploring
Will be to arrive where we started
And know the place for the first time.

Welcome to my world.

1. June 10, 2020

Samara said, there is a garden, your Garden. It is the place you arrive each time you visit the Middle World, and through it you access the other Worlds. Among much else that may be found there, you may meet the Animals and other entities who are your Spirit Guides. Spirit Guides are not the same thing as Power Animals. They do not augment your personal power, but rather assist and protect you in the three Worlds. During a career of Journeying there, you may accumulate a large number of them.

On June 10, 2020, Samara Journeyed to retrieve my Power Animal. She read me her notes about it the next day.

> *Went into my Garden and asked for an ally to come forward. Then I asked for Seth's spirit/dream self to enter. We walked to the healing space by the pump well and I told him to sit there and wait for me. Then Albert Einstein appeared and I was happy to see him. We walked down the cement ramp out of the barn, dove into the marsh creek, then dissolved through dirt, landing in the Lower World dark cave. We walked together and I noticed a small stream or brook running through the center of the cave. Then it opened from the darkness into a bright white cavern, with many stalagmites and stalactites in white and yellow. There was a quartz bench*

and we sat there. We looked into the water and saw koi, bright orange fish, and a green eel swimming by. Then a black bat flew in, groomed itself, then flew away. We waited patiently. Then a large black bear appeared with two little cubs behind her. This was your Power Animal, as it appeared 3 times. They slowly walked past me, then I asked the mother bear to stop because I needed to bring their power back to Seth. She said all of her power was also in her babies, so I could hold them. I picked the one up closest to me. It was about 25 pounds with wiry hair that was thick and soft. I hugged the bear to my heart and it wrapped its front paws on my neck and licked my face. I brought her energy into my heart. Then Albert and I journeyed back to the Garden the same way we had come and walked to you. You stood up and I sent the power of the Black Bear Power Animal into your solar plexus, your belly, where your power resides. Then we hugged and even more power came into your heart. We thanked Albert for helping us, and then I brought you back through the veil.

2.

It had started with a request for help with a homework assignment. My friend Samara said she was learning about shamanism. The assignment was to find someone's Power Animal.

Samara and I were attorneys in the Vermont Attorney General's Office. An invitation to participate in a shamanic quest for a Power Animal may seem an odd thing to receive from a fellow lawyer, but Samara was not your ordinary government bureaucrat. Describing her to friends, I tended to wax rhapsodic. Onto a solid substrate of northern Minnesota farming stock is laminated an improbably variegated history of vocations, interests, and abilities. She was, at the time in question, an eternally hopeful and eternally frustrated romantic, full of self-knowledge, wild and passionate experience, and stories to tell. Despite a path through life containing more than average turbulence, she navigates steadfastly and with good cheer, operating at an energy level several megawatts higher than that of most people. "More than average" is a phrase that comes up a lot, in relation to Samara. She can seem larger than life, dazzling. A broad smile frequently lights her round face and its mane of tawny hair. I often came away from our meetings feeling a bit like the Wallace Shawn character at the end of the evening in the movie "My Dinner with Andre": pleasantly weary, relaxed, and cautiously inspired.

Samara and I had been taking lunch together regularly for several years before I retired in 2017. At that time, we had agreed to continue to get together once a month. Unlike many such resolutions, this one held.

I was not one to decline the offer of a Power Animal, not if it came from Samara, even if I had only the vaguest notion of what a "Power Animal" might be. You can tear your eyes away from the winged seeds that are her namesakes as they twirl through the air, falling from the trees, but why would you want to?

Thinking later about Samara's invitation, and what ensued, this poem came to me:

Three months into a world locked down for
fear of things so tiny you can't see them
out of season a whirling jenny
helicopters near and calls to me

3.

With takeout cartons from a nearby cafe, we met for breakfast in the deserted office building where we had worked before my retirement and before the covid lockdown. The "stay home and stay safe" phase of the pandemic had passed recently in Vermont, but ongoing uncertainty about the disease's deadliness and transmissibility still made every visit to an indoor, public space an existentially thrilling adventure. The few restaurants still open served only to go. However, it would be a long time before state employees were called back to the office. Samara and I had the place to ourselves.

The rectangular atrium was several stories tall, huge and airy. Skylights ran its length. In this shoebox of shiny, grey and whitish stone, we sat at a little scattering of tables about halfway down the hall from the entrance's glass doors. At the far end from the entrance, along the left wall a staircase rose to a walkway on the second floor that connected the building's two office wings. Nobody appeared on the walkway the whole time we were there.

A janitor, then a security guard crossed the atrium floor and disappeared into unmarked doors. We put on our masks for them until we were alone again. It felt daring and exhilarating to sit and converse bare-faced.

A woman in full business suit, heels, makeup, and coifed hair erupted through the double doors at the entrance, marched the length of the atrium along the wall opposite us without glancing in our direction, climbed the stairs with quick, purposeful strides, and passed out of sight. We donned our masks for her, too. Samara said that the woman was a high-level official who attended the office every day like this, all alone, garbed in her power duds.

That was all the company we had, during the several hours we sat there, talking.

The teacher who had given Samara her "homework assignment," she explained, was named Wendy Halley, a psychotherapist and shamanic healer trained in native Hawaiian traditions. My innate skeptic reflexively suggested that I ask whether Wendy herself was native Hawaiian, but I refrained. I was here to help Samara, not to test the provenance of her teacher's ideas. Besides, I wanted my Power Animal, whatever that was.

However, I was not going to get a Power Animal, as it turned out, without also receiving a conceptual framework in which to fit it. From what Samara said, I gathered that a person is a triune entity, a composite of three Souls. There is the Body Soul, which operates largely below the level of consciousness; its domain is that of our physicality and emotions. The Mental Soul, corresponding roughly to the ego, organizes perceptions and directs activity. The Spirit Soul partakes of immortality and extrapersonal sources of wisdom, and is our true, essential being.

My reaction was, in retrospect, telling. I tried to find analogues to these ideas that were already familiar to me. I thought, "Father," thought of James Joyce's "ineluctable modality of the visible." I thought of Jewish mysticism and its nefesh (the animal soul), ruah (mentation and will), and neshamah (the immortal, upper soul). All this instead of just taking in what was being said, on its own terms.

Samara went on: corresponding to the three Souls are three Worlds. These Worlds are not worlds apart from or other than the world we live in. They are not alternative or parallel universes. Another way of putting it might be that just as a person is a compound of three Souls, our world is a compound of three Worlds. Each World expresses an aspect of the total reality within which a person exists, an aspect different from but related to the others. In the Lower World, the traveler finds Spirits expressive of natural phenomena and forces, animals, emotions, archetypes and other transpersonal phenomena rooted in the earth and in our relationship to physical existence. The Middle World expresses a person's mentality, taking the perceptions, abstractions, and narratives our consciousness constructs and reifying them as an environment of terrain, things, and inhabitants. The contents of the Middle World correspond to the contents of the world in which ordinary consciousness believes it resides. In the Upper World, your Upper Soul resides among great teachers, guides, spiritual masters, and angelic beings.

The Upper World sounded like a snore to me. Conversely, although Samara emphasized that the Lower World is not in any sense hell or an inferno, it still sounded scary. (Sure, convince me there aren't any vicious beasts or demons down there.) The Middle World was the one I found attractive. It was the most comfortable. The most familiar. Tell me more about me! Said my ego.

Samara said that her assignment was to go to the Lower World, find my Power Animal, and bring it back to me.

What is a Power Animal, I asked.

Samara said that a Power Animal, as the name implies, brings strength. It bolsters the person to whom it is attached.

And now Samara gave me an assignment. "In order for me to find your Power Animal, I need to know where you are weak. Tell me. Tell me the source of this weakness. Locate for me a point at which you are involuntarily vulnerable to the world. Describe what impairs your relationship with your higher self."

Damn! I'd thought she was going to do all the heavy lifting, not me. I was glad she'd brought doughnuts.

Later, thinking over our conversation in that large void between the workplace's walls of stone and glass, this poem came to me:

high heels'
echoes fill
the box
covid emptied
briefly stilling
our chatter
our thoughts
escape outside
the box

4.

Respect demanded that I give Samara's question a serious answer. Indeed, some version of her question had been on my mind for a while. I wrote to her as follows:

"I spend all day every day in a state of outrage. Every morning when I wake up, almost my first thought is a hope that the president died during the night. I don't much care how he died. I rather hope it was painful. I don't condone violence, but I would not much mind if someone lacking my scruples were to do it. My recurring fantasy is to meet him alone: I'm carrying a Louisville slugger. The first thing I do every day is to peruse the headlines in the *New York Times*. I invariably am disappointed not to read of the president's demise.

"I don't like any of this. This is not the person I want to be. It is not the person I was prior to November, 2016, at least, not most of the time.

"I was born on the banks of that great stream of non-religious Eastern European Jewish immigration to the United States, which blessed us with so many socialists and labor leaders and civil rights activists, including my maternal and paternal grandparents, just where it branched into the intellectual professions such as my parents followed. I was born seven years after the liberation of Auschwitz. My parents owned a hardbound copy of William L. Shirer's history of the Third Reich. On the dust jacket, on the spine, was a swastika. They had to hide it when my grandparents visited, because the sight of it would be so upsetting to them. I don't know how old I was when I first saw photographs from the concentration camps, emaciated survivors standing in rows and staring expressionlessly at the camera, piles of contorted corpses I had to look at twice before I could take in that they were human, but I am fairly certain it was long before my Christian schoolmates were confronted by such images, if ever they were. The Holocaust was central to my childhood identity as a Jew, more so than God, the Torah, Israel, or Sholem Aleichem, and reckoning with it became central to my larger identity as a human being.

"I grew up with a literally visceral aversion to bigotry, oppression, dishonesty, authoritarianism, and the violence the powerful and wealthy wreak on everyone else.

"They make me sick. I am a socialist and a supporter of labor unions, partly as a matter of ideology, but mainly from the pit of my stomach. My rage against Donald Trump and his minions is related to these things, and is rooted as well in fears I learned as a child. First, they come for the Jews. They will know who you are, whatever you do, and there's no place to hide.

"I do not want to be a fearful child in the world."

After sitting with these thoughts for a while, my memory

forcefully brought before me a poem I had written in 1990 about my paternal grandmother:

The Baube

As cruel as a small child who
slaps you in the face
to hear the sound it makes,
cruel as this music breaking through,
cruel is this new life, this new world!

House of Prayer, of Study, of Assembly:
Abode of Work, of Food and Love and Sleep:
Home of the Shabbos and Its short peace:
only one of these was *mine*,

or so whispered the air I breathed
as a small child in crowded streets, and
though I shut my ears to much,
I could not shut my nose.
All through those later, shining days

I scrubbed floors on my knees
because my man, a Commie Yid,
could not find work ("no bread, no Torah"
as it is said, as it is said),

wherever he left me was my place.
Shall I wail at the bitterness?
Pesach horseradish doesn't come close.
Of course, I kvetched at him whom the g-d
we'd lost faith in had given dominion.

Later yet, I told the children's children
over and over how wonderful, how bright
my only, my own, my one true doing—
they!—my accomplishments were.

They would not rest their eyes on me,
as if I were praising them unjustly,
as if I were praising them at all,
as if they wished I would shut up.
Perhaps they sensed which House laid claim

through my age-gullied lips,
and rightly—oh, rightly, my cruel ones!—
feared: they, who breathe
so easily this clean, free air

and open their ears the wider to hear
the songs it carries of hatred
of houses with closed doors,
houses they enter only to leave.
Among them I have no place.

5.

Samara was not the first person whose mind and values I respected who had presented me with beliefs that, upon first blush, might have struck me as bizarre. I was a non-religious, socialistically inclined Jew living in a society dominated by Christians, capitalists, and individualists. Negotiating an environment of alien worldviews was my way of life. Some years earlier, after my marriage had dissolved, I had dated a devoutly Greek Orthodox woman, one of the most keenly intelligent and rational people I have known. She had asked me to join her in an eternity of communion with Jesus. We were so compatible in so many other ways, I had struggled mightily to discover some means of integrating her religious worldview with my lack of same. In the end, it was painfully hopeless. But the process had only deepened my appreciation of her spirituality, and to the same degree had broadened and deepened my own perception of these matters. My inability to share hers did not invalidate it.

So, having dipped my toes into Samara's universe, I had eagerly waited to see what it would bring me.

This poem, written in 1996 during my marriage, before my encounter with Greek Orthodoxy, still expressed my basic attitudes about religious spirituality as of mid-2020:

An Agnostic Reads the Book of Psalms[1]

1

The psalmist, given by his life to know
to whom he owes it and the way, oh God,
to address his support and chief repose
in clear and simple agony of longing,

sings past my hearing. All his higher notes
are lost on me. At what he so devotes
his voice, I cannot say, although his words
may cross my lips more easily, perhaps, than

[1] Published in *Many Mountains Moving*, Vol. V, No. 1, "Literature of Spirituality" Special Edition, Spring 2002.

he from whom they were wrenched could emit them.
I pause only at what I do not know:
the meaning, not the words. They seem so much
the same one poem to the next, each dreary

hysteric plea to crush whoever seeks
the psalmist ill, each child-like, prattling praise
to Whom spring grass, the sky and vengeance all
are due; these words won't sink beneath the surface,

they bob and float before my eyes as light
and dead as balsa logs. I cannot bridge,
the way he does, this living river with
such forms of plea and praise. Swimming,

unsure of touching *terra firma*, sure
alone of someday touching bottom where,
profundis, he has also been, I hope
the water each stroke fills my palms with also,

as his last breaths led upward, filled his lungs,
and that the light he then saw is the one
that, broken on the flowing cusp of each
elusive wave, my eyes can't put together.

2

The god who could permit the Holocaust
is that same one who ordered Canaan cleared
of all its people. Broken light, that crossed
between the slats in cattle cars, as hard to

collect into coherent vision as
those blood-splashed desert rocks that not yet flowed

with milk and honey. Boggle at despair?
The note that strained the psalmist's throat yet higher

was just this one. It drove his faith's escape.
But if my bubble bursts before it finds
the sky, is it my fault? I might have been
recast as soap, that disappears in water,

that scrubbed a moral dullard shining pink,
all melted, leaving just a film a brush
would scour and somewhere else a name
a manifest preserves, no more, soiled paper,

an entry of the People of the Book,
no more. My faith would be no matter, then.
That Florentine who found a place for Jews
in heaven, found his faith's firm proof in spirit

discerned by him to flow from testaments
both old and new, that proved itself (he thought)
by turning the world Christian. Sorry sight.
Where Canaan wept, then Jews wept for their mercy.

Perhaps only a god could limn the world
so like as it is set in Torah: YHWH
(as we transliterate the name who've lost
the way to shape in breath its living vowels)

if I could see the hand that held the pen
at work in what the pen describes, and not
mere words so faithful to the facts they match,
I'd grant to you this life I hold so barely.

3

I do not seek to strike a bargain. Who
is there to bargain with? Who'd dicker with
his life? Not even David at his lyre
sought more than explanation or assurance.

Child of my time, I pose my hopeful wish
in terms not distant from the elegant
brutality we put to nature in
our science: show me what to build belief of.

Such questions beggar god, whose residence
is what we do not know. All consciousness,
a "neural darwinist" explains, derives
from shapes the brain cells grow to form their web and

the strength each gains to send its news and goods
across each synapse, wide as Hellespont:
at some, whole fleets of ferries haul freight trucks,
pedestrians, and cars; at others, beached, its

oars grey and feathered, oarlocks red with rust,
a dinghy collects rain. And "*qualia*,"
"beyond all explanation," he terms what
the poem carries from the lonely confines

of one poor Yorick to another, lost
to scientific reason because fleet
beyond all capture and unique; but here
and undeniable the dinghy shifts as

you settle on its battered bench and press
it deeper, gliding through encircling fog,
the vividly corroded, creaking pins
twin fulcra of your seemingly gainless motion

around which you, off center, pull and gasp
and sense, although you cannot say, just what
this boat is that you ride, and what the cool,
uncolored medium your oars kick swirls in.

4

When Dante, having trekked at reason's heels
through hell, arrived at paradise and left
that guide behind, he did not find at first
the woman who would take him on to heaven.

Instead, he walked a while beside a stream
with someone whose benignity surpassed
all doubt, though a stranger. Perhaps I, too,
am wandering an interval consigned to

the love of one I hardly know until
I am delivered over to that state
beyond our need for oxygen. That one
could be myself. In sole company, on

unsteady feet last summer wading in
a rocky-bottomed river, tea-red
waters that spilled through spindly pines packed dense
as felt, I flicked my bright green line and landed

my feathered hook with grace to drift in sync
among the other floating bugs and bits
of forest this and that right over where
there were no fish, and never have felt closer

in life so far to something that could be
acceptance of existence wholly bound
to matter *or* suffused with deity,
suspended between both in pressing currents.

As it is written, god, when queried, said
that we may tell the true from false among
those claiming prophecy to be their gift
by seeing what among the things predicted

has come to pass. Empirical, this test:
when no vibration, fast or slow, that quakes
on my tympanic membrane sounds in me,
in me a theory will have found, at last, rest.

6.

When Samara told me about the Journey my letter had inspired, about her encounter with Mama Bear and the cubs, I realized that this was many levels above a newspaper horoscope, or those paper placemats one sometimes gets in Chinese restaurants telling you that you have certain characteristics because you were born, say, in the Year of the Rat. Nothing like that. There was the story of her quest, beautiful in every detail, so strongly evocative of a lived reality—the space by the pump well, the barn and its cement ramp, the route to the underworld! the quartz bench! the cub's heft! its "wiry hair that was thick and soft"! Even more powerfully, I was impressed by the utter aptness of the image Samara brought me—the legendary protective ferocity of a Mama Bear, and the playful insouciance of her cubs! I thought it spoke to every dimension of my need.

I was thrilled and surprised, having in fact expected something on the order of a squirrel or a hummingbird. I did not need to surrender my reflexive skepticism about the validity or nature of Samara's gift, to enjoy receiving it. My ego preened at being associated with something so large and elementally powerful as a bear, as a whole family of bears! Even though this constituted somewhat of a misunderstanding, since after all the Power Animal isn't an alter ego, instead it makes up for deficiencies in one's personal power, still, I had the big guns on my side.

The little fellow in the back of my mind, so terrified of Trumpist Nazis, evidently agreed that the solidity, competence, and confidence of a Mama Bear, the indomitable, fearless, utterly ferocious abandon with which she protects her young, and the cubs' playful, freely affectionate, unthreatened engagement with the world, were just what we had needed. He breathed a sigh of relief, dropped his hysteria, and handed back responsibility for defending us to me, the one who can call on muscles, bulk, fangs, claws, and cunning. My transition from sleep to waking became less haunted, more benign.

The whole thing might have ended right there, as a gratifying and mildly exciting lark with a friend. At this point, learning about shamanism was for me indistinguishable from learning about Samara. She was onto something interesting, no doubt. I could have followed her into it vicariously.

Hush a bye, don't you cry,
Go to sleepy little baby.
When you wake you will have
All the pretty little horses.[2]

7.

But something like a fermentation had begun within me. Eventually, it bubbled over into the next step.

So far in my life, the spiritual teachings that had most appealed to me, apart from the elements of Jewish tradition that I had imbibed as it were with my mother's milk, were the teachings of Tibetan Buddhism as filtered through the popularizer Pema Chodron. I especially liked Buddhism's experiential nature. It did not require me to believe in anything. (My mother, as it happens, had told me when I was young that there was no reason a Jew couldn't be also a Buddhist, for this very reason.) Buddhist teachings relied for their validation not upon faith but upon my experience of the world. They offered me a mental technique, that is, meditation, with which I could strengthen, clarify, and contextualize that experience. Likewise, from what Samara was telling me, shamanism doesn't require me to believe anything that I can't corroborate from experience. It was a bit hard to see how this could apply to such things as dissolving through the dirt beneath a marsh creek, but let that go. The main points, as I then understood it, seemed to be that shamanism centered upon a specialized mental skill set with which one could generate experiences that extended one's understanding of the world and one's place in it; and that shamanism offered

2 Traditional lullaby. Joan Baez's rendition on her 1968 album "Baptism" is unforgettable.

a conceptual framework within which these experiences might occur, and which might be corroborated by them, but the framework was not required for the experiences to occur and its corroboration was in no way mandatory. This attracted me.

Another, hitherto mostly quiescent strain in my spiritual autobiography also now began to work. The best way to describe it, I think, is to tell you about an incident that had happened sixteen years previously, on a trip I had taken by car to Newfoundland with my then thirteen-year-old son.

Our family, still intact, had a tradition of "boys-only-camping-trips," which Isaac and I both cherished, as did the women in the family, probably for similar reasons. It was an opportunity for same-gender bonding within the family unit. On this trip, I wanted to visit L'Anse Aux Meadows, site of the first known Viking settlement in North America, predating Columbus by five hundred years. It is at the far northern tip of that desolately beautiful island, several days' drive from the dock on the southern coast where the ferry from Nova Scotia drops you off.

On the way north, we stopped at Gros Morne National Park. In Gros Morne is a place called the Tablelands. It is a treeless area of orangish, five hundred-million-year-old rock that was forced from the earth's mantle to the surface when tectonic plates collided and the Appalachian Mountains were thrust up. Eroded over four hundred million years, the part of the Tablelands that I visited consists of two gently rounded arms extending from the plateau that embrace a u-shaped valley with a little stream running through it. From the parking area, a boardwalk carries you around the tip of one of the arms, to the stream. From there you can follow a dirt trail along the stream into the valley, about two kilometers from where you left your car.

It was a mildly overcast, chilly day, threatening rain and hypothermia. Isaac and I had the parking area to ourselves. Engrossed in his Game boy, he politely expressed a lack of interest in wandering into this barren, almost featureless landscape, so I left him in the car. For my part, I love this kind of place.

I walked all the way along the very gently sloping, almost level trail, meeting no one. After twenty minutes or so, I stood in the valley. Nothing there but me, the clouds, the stream, the ancient, ancient rocks. It had that kind of stillness that is anything but. I stood there for what seemed like a long while, communing with I knew not what.

About halfway back to the car, nearing the boardwalk, I came upon a stone in the middle of the path. It had not been there before. The path had been perfectly clear. I had remarked to myself how well maintained it was. I couldn't imagine how the stone had gotten there. I had seen no other people in the parking lot or anywhere else. No ledge or cliff was near enough for the stone to have rolled here from it or to have been thrown here from above. The stone was too big to have been dropped by anything but the largest bird, leaving aside why a very large bird would be flying around with such an impediment and the fact that I had seen no such animal. Likewise, I'd seen no sign of any mammal large enough to have moved it, assuming it would have wanted to.

The stone appeared reddish-orange with grey-green veins, like the Tablelands from which it came. It is a bit bigger than a human heart, but the same shape; it resembles the actual organ, not a valentine. After contemplating it for what seemed like a long time—duration was hard to estimate, in that place—I decided that however it had gotten to its present location, the stone was somehow meant for me to find.

I remembered a story I had read about a Native American shaman. I don't recall the tribe. A white man asked him, "Is it true that you can talk with rocks?" He said, "Yes, it's easy, but you have to know which ones." It seemed to me that this probably was one of the ones. I picked it up and took it home.

For the past sixteen years, I had wanted to learn how to talk with that stone. It wasn't a burning desire by any means, and I would have been the first to acknowledge that it wasn't exactly a rational ambition, but "the heart has reasons. . . ."

I asked Samara to teach me how to Journey.

During the five ensuing months, I processed my feelings, thought my thoughts, dealt with the advent of the coronavirus, waited for an opportunity to get together safely with Samara, and carved a piece of scrap cherry wood into a little Mama Bear. It's the wrong color, since she is a black bear, but cherry is what I had lying around, not ebony. For cubs I used two porcelain figurines I had gotten in boxes of the Red Rose Tea I'd consumed many cups of every day over my years of legal practice. They are just the right size to reach her teats.

One year later, thinking back on my trip with Isaac, I wrote this poem:

Tablelands

I have seen my mother's bones,
naked, shattered, immense,
and the waters threading down them
braided at my feet
and rushed through the rubble
calling loudly.

8. November 11, 2020

Toward the end of those five months, Samara prepared me for my first visit to my Garden. She gave me procedural guidelines. I should have my Power Animal close by. (No problem there. I had my carving of Mama Bear, the figurines of her cubs.) I should put in my earbuds, for listening to the recording of shamanic drumming that she had given me. I should lie down, with a blanket handy to keep me warm. I should cover my eyes, to keep out light that would distract me from the trance and anchor me on this side of the "veil" that separates ordinary reality from what is experienced in trance. (I had an eye pillow, plus some blackout shades that I used to wear when I was married and my wife liked to read at night. I chose the eye pillow.) I should take a deep breath, relax my body, then click on the drumming and let the trip begin. After it ends, I should write down a description of everything I experienced. I should do this as soon as possible, because otherwise it would fade from memory, as all but the most vivid dreams will do. I should make drawings, if that might help recollection. I should note directions.

Online research supplemented Samara's guidelines with the suggestion that I should begin by visualizing walking from my bedroom to the front door of my house, outside, and through the veil, returning the same way when the drumming changes rhythm and tempo.

Samara told me that everything I would encounter in the Garden is symbolic of me or of my life experience. Everything can be communicated with. I could change things in the Garden. For example, she had cleared a field in her Garden with a bulldozer. But I should be careful about making changes. Before doing so, I should ask the thing that I am thinking of changing why it is there and what it represents. It is important to investigate in this manner before acting, because if I were to change something in the Garden, something would change correspondingly in my "regular" life. Finally, written in capital letters at the bottom of my notes, is the injunction, LOOK AROUND. WHERE IS THIS GARDEN CONNECTED TO?

The appointed day arrived. Samara and I met briefly that morning via Zoom for a preflight check-in. We had agreed to Journey simultaneously and to Zoom together again afterwards, to compare notes.

All systems go. The drumming was both resonant and soothing, monotonous, insistent. I couldn't not listen to it. I began to hear the ghosts of rudimentary tunes in the overtones. My mind began to wander:

> *Overshadowing the whole thing, from beginning to end, is fear of not being able to find my way back.*
>
> *At first, chaotic lights and darkness, indistinguishable from the phantasms that normally flit behind closed eyelids. Flashing, vague forms. I try hard to visualize the bedroom to hallway to front door to outside route that the web site prescribed, but I can't do so in a clear and continuous fashion. It comes fragmented, in pieces, not consecutive. I arrive at a wall of seemingly impenetrable blackness several times. I begin to doubt that I ever will arrive in the Garden. I persist, enter the darkness, feel my way through. It might be accurate to say that I push my way through, except that the resistance is not physical. It lightens to a dense, purplish fog or mist. I feel I am inside a cloud, trapped within the veil between worlds, unable to break through.*

I start to get sharp, very clear glimpses, as if through gaps in the cloud, of brilliant, deep blue sky and dense, green foliage. Was it an evergreen? The glimpses are too quick to be sure. A huge tree, that much was certain. Am I under it? I sense that I'm looking mostly upwards.

I can't push through the purple fog. Every time I feel about to break through to the other side, a pang of fear stops me. Several times I visualize my body lying in my bedroom, just to reassure myself that I can return to it. At those times, the cloud thickens to black. After a few repetitions of this, I learn to turn from it, to stay where I am in the lighter, purple zone that allows me glimpses of what I am sure is my Garden. I practice waiting, not trying to control the vision, letting it bring itself to me.

I call on Mama Bear to help me.

I make out vague forms beyond the mist, not in it. I have no sense of direction and little control over where I am looking.

No: I am looking upward, at the sky! The sky is covered entirely with a sheet of light lavender clouds.

I see a few flashes of some sort of building. A two- or three-story house? A peaked roof? A gable? I see more tree foliage, but now it is definitely deciduous, in fall colors.

Then, my field of vision darkens. At first, I think that the cloud/veil has deepened around me again, but looking more closely, I realize that instead I am looking downward at rich, dark soil. If I were seeing with my eyes, I would say that they now lift to graceful, curving blades of grass, very close up, as if I were lying on my stomach on a tall, uncut meadow. Visions of fern fronds alternate with the grass blades, like a repetitious slide show. This dissolves to a steady, full view of a huge tree, presumably the one I first saw. The tree is a little dark and blurry, as if viewed through a camera lens stopped down too far and poorly focused. A white pine, I think.

The drumming stutters, signaling that the Journey is coming to an end. I withdraw into my form lying on the bed, feeling light, calm, and centered.

It took a few minutes to make my notes. Back in Zoom, Samara had been waiting for me a little while when I returned. The first thing I was aware of, seeing her face on the screen, was that something about her skin, the way it draped her bones, told me she was in a state of relaxation similar to mine.

9. November 14, 2020

My next attempt got me no further.

Failure to get beyond the black curtain. No purple mist, even. For a while, broken images, fleeting, mostly too rapid or fragmented or indistinct to recognize. Through a jagged, tiny opening in the black—like a moth hole in a sweater—one glimpse of the big tree. A clear and somewhat lasting vision of green leaves. Beech leaves? Teardrop-shaped, with smooth margins. From very close, a brief glimpse of some sort of insect, its body a brilliant, intricate pattern of yellow and black—a monarch butterfly caterpillar? Yes, that's what it is. A dark, reflective surface—water? Glass? A cat's eye.

Sadness, at the end. There had been a few moments, particularly when I was seeing the tree and the leaves, when I'd felt that the Garden was about to open to me, and at those same instants I'd felt a physical jolt, like fear but not quite fear, reminiscent of something I'd felt when I was learning to ride a motorcycle and the thought would come to me that I might fall and I would squeeze the brakes convulsively, which ironically almost did make me lay the bike down. Only much later did it occur to me what caterpillars traditionally signify.

This poem, written almost on the same date as the event it describes, captures the sadness I'm talking about, a frustrated yearning:

March 9, 1992

odd how distant this afternoon's
brief sojourn on that bridge
seems I stood staring the voices
walking by behind me made me
uncomfortable momentarily
thinking they would think me
odd at least to gaze so fixedly
upstream to the next bridge
beneath which puddles had formed
on the rotting ice but I
recalled how Yeats met his
illuminating moment
in a cafe surrounded by
unwitnessing witnesses
so reflected on the ice's
sheets from each bank meeting
at midstream meltwater runnel
that grooved deeply the
grey-green mottled slickening
surface eating at spots
through the plates to dark
unstill abodes of slowly breathing

fish almost overwintered
but the glaring blessing hung
back of the next bridge's
brown arches and the shops
and cars atop it and the ice
simply slowly melted but
would not melt for me away

10.

I might have understood my own vision better, if I'd taken the little bit of its imagery that I could understand as seriously as I'd taken Samara's question. If so, I might have behaved differently. Instead, I worried about what I might have done wrong. I thought maybe my ego was getting in the way.

My meditation practice over the years had provided me with copious examples of ego's predilection for creating distractions from perceptions that threaten to reveal just how limited ego's domain is. In the early days, after a few minutes of sitting I would get mysteriously sleepy, heavy-eyed and yawning no matter how well rested I actually was. In a later phase, about midway through most meditation sessions I would see small, colored lights, like Christmas tree lights, dancing across my field of vision, entrancingly pretty. What were they? Worried that this might be a mild hallucination indicating something wrong with me (it's a theme), I asked my meditation teacher about it. The jokester said, "It's enlightenment." The phenomena ceased after I learned to let them go, to not feed them with attention. But yet there were itches, and occasional muscle spasms in my feet, and the urge to look at the clock and see how much time was left, and always, always, the almost unceasing whirl of thought, in which ego can be detected chasing its own tail, like a cat at play. All things considered, stabs of mild panic shouldn't be outside ego's repertoire.

Even on the basis of my very limited experience of trance, it was clear to me that it is not the same thing as meditation, but it also seemed clear that the two are related, at the very least in the disciplined quietness with which the practitioner must approach them, and in their orientation outside and beyond that which we conventionally consider belongs to our self. I reasoned: if the ego perceives a well-conducted meditation practice as an assault, so, too, may the shamanic Journey cause it to engage its defenses. After all, if the Journey reveals anything at all, it is a world other than the one the ego knows.

Perhaps, I thought, the best way to get me out of my way might be through ritual. Ritual is a form of prayer; prayer is a means of orienting oneself in correct relation to that aspect of existence which seems most salient to the moment. One doesn't need a deity to pray to, for prayer to have meaning. Ritual could help establish a setting conducive to the trance, like easing oneself into something that otherwise might be uncomfortable, like a hot bath or a cold mountain stream. Ritual could provide a firm and consistent base from which to proceed, like a quarterback setting his or her feet before throwing a long pass. Ritual could provide a framework, satisfying ego's need for orderly and controlled procedure.

I'd been reading about shamanism, surveying the terrain I was entering, wanting to do it right. Nearly all accounts described a more or less ritualistic approach to the Journey. The problem was, every culture in which shamanism was known to be practiced, of which there were astonishingly many, worldwide, had evolved its own characteristic methods and styles. The details of shamanism varied not only from culture to culture, but from shaman to shaman. One shaman has a rattle, and a robe made to exacting specifications at a certain time of year from the hide of a particular animal; the robe is covered with significant decorations, bangles, embroidery, painting; there's a headdress constructed ritualistically from the skull of yet another animal killed in a certain place using a sacred knife; and so on. Another does without the elaborate costume but draws elaborate diagrams in the dirt and intones prayers borrowed from a North American tribal tradition but invoking the Jewish divinity. Another seeks guidance from the Directions. The tradition I was being introduced to apparently required nothing more than to put in your earbuds, lie back, and relax. There is and apparently ever has been no one correct way, and no obvious reason to privilege one approach over another.

Right about this time, I encountered this quote from the ancient Roman orator Symmachus: "Whatever each person worships, it is reasonable to think of them as one. We see the same stars, the sky is shared by all, the same world surrounds us. What does it matter what wisdom a person uses to seek for the truth?"[3] Symmachus may or may not have pounded a drum, but for me he rang a bell. I would have to construct my own ritual, if I wanted it to speak to and for me.

The first thing I thought of was something I already had at hand. Ten or fifteen years ago, the desire had crept upon me to own a shofar, a horn taken from an antelope or ram that is used musically to punctuate certain Jewish ritual observances, said punctuation consisting primarily of an exclamation mark. As it is said, God used a shofar to get the Israelites' attention at Sinai, and David blew one to bring down the walls of Jericho. It is a powerful noise. But, being neither an observant Jew nor even a regular attendee at any synagogue, what use had I for such a thing? None. It just had begun to feel important to own one. Perhaps you have experienced

3 Quoted in Catherine Nixey, *The Darkening Age: The Christian Destruction of the Classical World* (Mariner Books 2017), p. 132

something similar. Something grows in your imagination, seeded there for no apparent reason or purpose. Perhaps it is a trip to Tahiti, or a leather handbag, or a dish your mother made of prunes and brisket, or a statuette of Kuan Yin, goddess of mercy. Children are prone to this. They have to have a slinky, or a kitten, or a chocolate pudding. It's not quite a craving, and not quite an obsession, more like an itch you increasingly feel you have to scratch.

For six months or so, I had researched shofars. There are several kinds, of several sizes, in several price ranges. I'd settled on the one I wanted. Ordering it online seemed wrong, somehow, so I'd visited a local synagogue. I'd described to the female Assistant Rabbi what I was looking for, and asked her help in obtaining it. Of course, I'd said, I would pay for it. She'd asked me why I wanted it. I had told her that I wasn't sure, that I felt drawn to it in a way that I couldn't explain, that I strongly wanted to learn to play shofar but I did not know to what end. A few weeks later, I had received a phone call from the temple, telling me that my shofar had come in.

It is a Yemenite shofar, fashioned from the horn of a kudu antelope, a brown and tan, loose spiral two and a half feet long. From scraps of cherry wood, I had carved a pair of brackets to hang it on my bedroom wall. For the time being, the itch had been scratched. There my lovely, clear-throated horn had remained mostly undisturbed except for dusting, until now. I would use it to call across the veil.

Thinking about my long-dormant shofar, this poem came to me. I spoke it aloud slowly, one line at a time, with ample silence after each utterance:

overwintering
chrysalis
digesting

itself
appears
motionless
sounds
unstirring

dangles
windblown
unshaken
within

11. November 16, 2020

A day to be marked with a star.

I lit a sage bundle and waved it about the room and around my body, enjoying its dry-sweet, musky scent.

I thanked the six Directions—north, south, east, west, up, and down—for what each of them brings and for giving me a space to exist, greeting each direction with the shofar. (Once you've heard the shofar's clear, penetrating, exultant summons, it's easy to imagine it calling to powers capable of destroying a city's stone fortifications!) I asked the Directions' support for my Journey to my Garden.

Using the shofar, I summoned Mama Bear and the cubs. I asked for their assistance and protection on my Journey.

I got in bed, put in my earbuds, started the drumming, and covered my eyes.

The bell of the shofar, the wider end that is, appealed to me as a possible portal through the veil. I began to picture myself diving into its swirling ochre and tan depths, its narrowing gyre, but before I even reached the rim:

Wham! I am there almost instantly, the Big Tree towering before me.

I tell myself, wait a second, I am supposed to enter through a portal and go through the veil; suddenly, I'm in the blackness, as if kicked back there by this thought. I go back and forth a couple of times (Big Tree . . . "but, portal!" . . . blackness . . . Big Tree . . . "but, portal!" . . . blackness) until I decide what the heck, accept it, here I am.

I am oriented in space. I am standing, looking at the Big Tree, a white pine, the most enormous white pine I have ever seen. It's directly in front of me, no, a bit to my left. I move towards it. As the Journey goes on, I get better and better at directing my movement through this place. It's mostly a volitional act, but tricky, because sometimes I just find myself somewhere without having consciously intended to go there. Now I am under the Tree. It's dark under here. Moving to the left, I enter a deciduous grove.

I am standing at one end of a long, narrow clearing in the grove. The sky is grey above me. At the far end of the grove is an ell-shaped house. A farmhouse? The shorter wing is two stories tall, and there is a porch on the long, one-story wing. There's light in the windows. It must be evening here, I think.

Continuing on to the left, I enter an open space. I am among tall grasses, overgrown, almost head high. I walk into the meadow. I come to a grassy mound. Is it a burrow? Farther away across the meadow, quite far away, stands a lone tree with a globular spread of foliage surmounting a tall, bare trunk. Lollipop-shaped. It is far enough away that I see it only indistinctly. I try to move towards this tree, but I make little progress.

So, I continue to circle to the left, and come back to the white pine, the Big Tree. In the dark beneath it, I see something.

I become aware of a difference between this Journey and the two previous ones. Despite Samara's advice to have no particular expectations, I had embarked upon the previous Journeys with the idea that my experience would in some way approximate watching a movie. There would be good production values, continuity, saturated colors, seamless special effects. I had strained after this, and had been disappointed by the generally monotone, low-resolution actuality. Up until this point, this Journey, too, has appeared as a similarly low-budget affair. The difference, then, is that I no longer am straining after sharply focused vividness. My attitude is to accept whatever is presented to me, and to interpret it as best I can.

Now, under the pine, I clearly see a ball of almost glowing, reddish-brown. A gleaming, dark eye, surrounded by this luminous, reddish-brown fur. A long, narrow, animal face looks directly at me, close to me. Is it Mama Bear? I ask if it's her, and feel joyful to think I might be meeting her. I say, don't leave me, Mama Bear. But Mama Bear is a black bear, so this isn't her. I think, it's a fox. It disappears, fading away.

I turn farther left. It becomes very dark. Unlike the darkness under the trees, which is textured, this is a smooth darkness. Geometric shapes, like the corners where walls meet, emerge from the darkness. A ceiling overhead. I realize that I am in the house. I know that I will return to the house someday, but right now I don't want to be there. It's a bit scary in there. I go outside.

I move back, away from the house, and see it more distinctly than before. Then I continue to the left, back out into the almost head high, overgrown grassland. I think, it needs to be mowed. I wander around, looking for the patch of bare earth I stared down into during my first Journey, and for the mound that might be an animal's burrow, but I can't find them before the drum tells me it's time to come home.

12.

It may not seem like much: trees, grass, a strange farmhouse, a small pile of dirt, a fox. What blew me away was the strong sense, amounting to a feeling of certainty, that all this exists in its own right, that none of it depends on "me" for its existence, that each of these things and all of them together represent a world through which I had passed and am passing.

I believe that feelings provide us with real, usable data about the world, despite their frequent ambiguity and unreliability, as real as the data of our five conventionally recognized senses, despite our inability to understand, explain, or even to detect them scientifically. I am not talking about "feelings" as a synonym for "emotions," although there is some overlap. Proprioception is a feeling. We may feel that someone likes or dislikes us, is truthful or a liar. We may feel that we are being watched, that it is unsafe to enter a room, that a storm is coming. We may experience déjà vu. We may wake up and feel that it is 3:30 a.m. We may feel that an animal encountered in the woods will not bite us if we behave in a certain way. I think of feelings as akin to sensory input. "Feeling" may be a sense in its own right, like proprioception, or perhaps it is a result of processing what we have detected through one or a combination of our other senses, including but not limited to the basic five. People vary in how keen their feelings are, how sensitive they are to them, how accurate their interpretation of their feelings may be. We do not have to believe literally what we think our feelings are telling us, in order to accept them as providing important data.

As a poet, I am familiar with the process of imaginative creation. I know when I've made something up, as opposed to when I am describing something that I did not make up. (Which is to say, in addition to being a poet, I'm sane. I also admit the possibility that my knowledge of this distinction is not infallible. Ditto.) But the Garden felt very much a case of something not originating in my imagination. Going there had not been a matter of entertaining a fantasy.

There is a mystery to authorship, maybe not for every writer, but for many of us. When you're really writing well, when you're "in the zone," it's as if the material is coming to you or through you, but not from you. It comes from "somewhere else." You see the things you're writing about as if they were placed in front of you by some agency other than you. Your job is not to create them, but to describe them. Characters say and do things that surprise you, that you couldn't have precited and wouldn't have invented and definitely did not intend for them, speaking and acting like autonomous beings. You write down their sayings and doings because you know that those words and actions are as true to life as what your best friend said to you yesterday, and because you know that they are telling the story you were trying to tell better than you could tell it, even if they're taking it in a direction different from the one you had imagined. It's as if you're taking dictation, not, that is, the words themselves, at least not necessarily the words themselves, but the content of the words.

The Garden, I felt, is like that, a place of living images. What relationship may those images bear to the images that constitute quotidian reality? Asking that question, I felt profoundly unstuck and discombobulated.

One response I had was to make a "to-do" list of things to follow up with on subsequent Journeys. I think it may have been Samara's suggestion to make such a list. This effort to organize the experience, to make an action plan from it, in essence to exert some control over it, is evidence of how deeply I had been shaken. The list was a very thin membrane interposed between "me," that is, on the one hand, the self I identify with from day to day among experiences that self believes to constitute the entirety of its habitation, and, on the other hand, the Garden's astonishing impact.

Back in 2004, I had written a poem that expresses in part the unsettled feeling I had at this time. The poem describes an experience I'd had, taking a perfectly ordinary walk on a perfectly ordinary country road, when the world threw me from it into another place that was still the world:

Catching Breath

If you are walking along a dirt road in the country,
facing where the traffic would come from if there were any,
and you carry your gaze unfocused over your right shoulder,
you will see the occasional oaks and maples across the lane
slip on by, and there in the middle of that wheeling field,
harsh white against the fresh plowed earth, a birch
around which it all seems to pivot, until the birch too
falls away, and things in the distance almost keep up,
that farmhouse out there, for example, you could walk an hour
and it would still be just within that part of the world
washed by your tears, but passing out of it; and looking

to your left it's the same, things nearby sliding by so fast,
and further out upon further out things nearly keeping up
with you, as if to the right and the left the wings of
the world
seek to close around you but instead you are ejected ahead,
and the only way you can stop it all is to stop. So, you hold
the crunch of the road beneath your feet. Everything's silent.
A car rushes by—you didn't see it coming, then it's gone.
A bumblebee zoops among the black-eyed susans by
the ditch,
that dip with its landing and rebound at lift-off. A bird
too far
away to identify says something. No, there are three,
drawing halos around the cloud that rides towards the
farmhouse.
The trees flutter in a breeze not strong enough to carry away
the mosquito that has found your left ear. Even that puddle
in the broad part of the ditch before the culvert is streaked
by waterbugs zipping and skating their inscrutable
purposes,
tout le monde pell mell relating space to time, the same
whether or not you add your own little movement. So,
not being dead, you have no choice. You must. You do.

13. November 19, 2020

Samara had told me it was important to establish the boundary of my Garden. I started by smudging to the six Directions, thanking them, asking their support for my Journey to the Middle World to explore my Garden and find its boundaries. But I went through the ritual in a hurried and mechanical manner, my mind not fully present. I almost forgot to circle myself with the sage's smoke. I blew the shofar to summon Mama Bear and the cubs, but my attention was on the merely performative aspects of the music.

I envisioned the shofar as portal, and—

Quickly, there's a white mist. Just as quickly, I am in the long clearing in the deciduous grove, at the far end from the house. I have little control over my spatial orientation or movement. No matter what I intend to do, I am moving towards the house. I have no feeling of being pulled or otherwise compelled in that direction, no sense of being subject to some overpowering force, it is just what is happening.

Then I am in the house. It's dark in here. Some sort of chandelier hangs from the ceiling, its many dangling crystals unlit. I feel scary chills, like "someone stepped on your grave." I don't want to be in here. I want to go outside. I try saying, "I'm outside," but it doesn't work. I wander through the dark, obscure rooms. I can't find a way out. I see windows, and through their panes I see trees. At last, I find a door ajar. I go through it.

I have come out the house's back door. I head into the woods behind it. There's a strong, sweet smell. It's dark. I don't know what I'm looking at, can't see well enough. I'm not sure where I am or which way I am going. I try to turn myself aside or around. The house begins to slide into view. I don't want to go there. I see, in the darkness, a gracefully curving red streak, thin as a hair, glowing. Then, two of them close together. Fox fur? An animal form begins to emerge from the dimness. I'm pretty sure it's the fox. "Who are you?" I ask. It fades away without answering.

All around me are obscure, unidentifiable shapes. That

is, I see rectangles, triangles, other geometric forms, but I don't know what they belong to. They are not natural, organic shapes, but they are not organized in any way I comprehend. Maybe they are piecemeal views of features of the house, its walls, its gable, its peaked roof? Maybe I'm walking around it, just outside it. The sweet smell is strong. Is it the sage I smudged with? No, it's much more like honeysuckle, not as strong as lilac or as spicy as roses. Maybe honeysuckle is planted around the house and I'm walking through or near it.

I become fairly sure, for no particular reason, that I have wandered back into the woods behind the house. The sweet smell disappears, then recurs several times. Now, it's accompanied by a dry, musky, animal smell. I decide that maybe this Journey is not about visual sensory input, and I should just follow my nose. I follow the sweet smell, trying to go towards it. For some reason, I don't even consider the possibility that this could take me back to the house. Though fully conscious, one's cognition works differently, on a Journey. Anyway, it doesn't take me there. A couple of times again I see those red, glowing filaments. I continue this way for a while, sometimes losing the sweet smell, sometimes picking up the dry, animal smell.

Then, just ahead to the right, stands a dark, rounded shape, about six feet tall. I have much more of the animal smell than the sweet smell at this point. But, it's not a bear. It's a shrub. At my feet is a sort of smooth blankness. Its exact border keeps shifting slightly. It is water. It could be flowing water, or it could be a pond. I can't see across. One thing seems certain. I have reached a boundary of my Garden.

The drum calls me home.

I ended this Journey in a confused state of mind. I wanted to understand everything that had happened, but it all seemed so vague, so muddy. In Jewish prayer and ritual, there is the concept of "kavanah," meaning the quality of mindful intentionality with which one performs the acts. Maybe this had been lacking in me? Maybe a simple declarative meaning was too much to ask for. On the other hand, maybe the dreamworld possesses its own intentionality; it certainly seemed to want me to visit the house and spend time in there! It even had granted my wish to visit the Garden's boundary. Maybe the dreamworld knows what it is doing, and the task of that part of me which I like to think of as "me", in visiting the dreamworld, was to learn to listen better.

14. November 23, 2020

Having plunged into this new world, I felt as much bewilderment as excitement. How to go about exploring it?

Samara had told me of a workbook that her teacher, Wendy Halley, had created to help people find their way into the dreamworld. I bought it.

The workbook[4] is a slender volume, consisting mainly of a series of exercises designed to carry the novice progressively deeper into the art of Journeying. My first impressions upon opening it were favorable. It is neither scholarly nor formal, but speaks with the author's considerable personal authority. She writes in colloquial prose, with clarity, simplicity, and common sense, if "common sense" may properly be applied to an engagement with dreamlike trance states that is the

4 Wendy S. Halley, *The Magical Path: Conscious Dreaming Exercises for Healing & Growth* (Lucid Path Healing Arts 2010)

province, in the modern Western world, of a very small fringe minority. Her book demonstrates that a modern practitioner, not born to a living shamanic tradition but having been introduced to it indirectly, can write about shamanism without the taint of cultural appropriation, acknowledging the sources from which her understanding derives without pretending a closer identification with them than is warranted. As time went on, I became increasingly happier with my purchase. It provided the plan, the framework that my quotidian self so needed to cling to, for encountering the dreamworld, integrating and learning from what I found there without having it shatter my shaking sense of reality.

Also, there was something comforting about having a printed guide, physical evidence in my hands that I was engaging in activities belonging to a community. Already, I was beginning to feel the social isolation that comes with doing something that one feels to be important but that is so far outside the mainstream that there is no easy way to talk with nearly anyone about it without running up against massive ignorance and preconceptions. My own ignorance and preconceptions were proving hard enough to deal with! Not to mention the lack of commonly understood terminology with which to describe these experiences. The workbook, just by existing, alleviated all that. That it also would turn out to be useful in practice, as indeed it did, was a hoped-for but almost unexpected benefit.

One of the early exercises in the workbook involves visualizing a bird, "hopping on the bird's back and going for a spin."

I asked the Directions, my Spirit Helpers (whoever they may be), and Mama Bear to support and protect me in my Journey to the Middle World to find a bird to fly me around my Garden. I forgot to include the cubs. I found it difficult to visualize the shofar's bell, so I just went with whatever was going to happen.

Lots of colors in the darkness, reds and purples and deep blues, very vivid and saturated. Well, I say to myself, you've been complaining about things being monochromatic. Flashes of light, sometimes white, sometimes colored. None of it coalesces into anything recognizable, despite the frequent sense I have of being on the verge of that happening. Several times I have the sense of being in the space on a bird's back between its wings, accompanied by an image that I can only describe in visual terms even though my eyes have not brought it to me, an image like a black-on-black painting in which even the finest details are clearly defined, every feather distinct, swelling before me to the bird's neck.

I follow a ribbed tunnel towards its lighter end. It twists gently around an axis, like (I realize later) the shofar.

I emerge from the tunnel into more, incoherent colors.

Suddenly, I see treetops. I'm skimming just over them. I am riding on a bird. I don't see the bird, but it's there. I ask the bird to take me over the grassy area of my Garden. "Nothing to see there," it replies. I ask it to take me to the top of the Big Tree, where we might perch for me to take in the view.

Colors, glimpses of a triangular or conelike treetop's branches against the bright, blue sky, nearby, not far above us.

I ask the bird to take me higher, where I can see everything, to take me into the light. No response. I ask the bird to show itself to me. It laughs and says, "Not until we land." Somehow, this makes sense.

More disorganized colors. Throughout the whole trip, I

am continuously conscious of the drum pounding away, and of my chest muscles that repeatedly tighten and have to be relaxed consciously.

At last, clearly and vividly, as if silhouetted against black velvet, I see a short, strong, curved, yellow beak; a black-masked bird's eyes; a red crest. I say, "You're a cardinal!"

"Yes," she says.

15.

After that explosive November, what had started as an amusing favor for a friend had become a major preoccupation. My sense of reality was shaken. What was I getting into? Being me, I tried to read up on it, groping for a context that would comprehend and reconcile these experiences and the world I'd thought I lived in.

It quickly became apparent that I could take this in several directions. There was a surprising amount of literature about shamanism, much of it from New Age types, for whom "indigenous wisdom" had become a thing in the past few decades. That seemed like a place to start. But a few forays into this vein of writing made it apparent that it wouldn't take me where I needed to go. For example, curious about the symbolism of the animals that had been showing up in my Journeys, I dipped into *Animal Speak: The Spiritual and Magical Powers of Creatures Great and Small*, by Ted Andrews. I bought the book because it contains a fairly comprehensive dictionary of animal symbolism and, from what I could glean online, Andrews had a lengthy track record of apparently sincere commitment to this and related subjects. He didn't seem to have been a huckster who just made stuff up. According to

Andrews, a cardinal "reflects a time to renew our vitality" through "lessons in developing and accepting a new sense of our own true self-importance." If female, it "reflects a need to assert . . . creativity and intuition more strongly."[5] Yeah, well . . . thanks. This seemed to relate to my experience in a very general but completely obvious way. It did not offer any insight or guidance as to how to relate to the cardinal, with her distinctive personality and clearly expressed sense of autonomous will, in any future encounters.

I was tempted to revisit the books of Carlos Castaneda, which were wildly popular during my high school and college years. In the first and most famous of them, *The Teachings of Don Juan: A Yaqui Way of Knowledge*, Castaneda, an anthropology grad student at UCLA, purported to describe his peyote-fueled apprenticeship with a Native American shaman, or "brujo," of the Yaqui tribe. For a few years, the books irrupted shamanism into American public consciousness. But anthropologists fairly unanimously have concluded that the books are works of fiction, written by someone ignorant of almost anything to do with the actual Yaqui, let alone their ways of knowledge.

Frustrated by the fluffiness and potential for falsehood of this strand of the literature, I turned to more academically respectable sources. And there I hit the motherlode: Mircea Eliade's *Shamanism: Archaic Techniques of Ecstasy*, all 600 pages of it. It became my reading material for the next several months, during which time I stayed well this side of the veil. The emotional and intellectual impact Eliade had on me would be hard to overstate, so I am going to spend a bit of time on it, here. A brief summary can only hint at the richness of this book.

5 Ted Andrews, *Animal Speak: The Spiritual and Magical Powers of Creatures Great and Small* (Lewellyn Publications 2020), p. 124.

First published in French in 1951 and then in English in 1964, *Shamanism* was the first comprehensive, scholarly examination of the subject. The thirteen-year gap between the two editions probably is evidence of the less-than-burning interest in shamanism in the English-speaking world at that time. Inevitably, there has been some criticism of the book in the seven decades since it appeared. It has been said, for example, that Eliade tended to overgeneralize, that he overlooked some parts of the globe and overemphasized others, and that his extensive reliance on anthropological source material is marred by his own lack of first-hand anthropological field experience. None of the criticism has disturbed his book's status as the closest thing we have to a definitive treatise, so far, unlikely to be superseded.

Due mostly to the unwieldy mass of material and detail that it contains, I found *Shamanism* something of a slog to read, but I persisted and could not put it down, because, well, it blew my mind. In a good way. Here was a perspective capacious enough to contain the disruptive force of my November Journeys, if not to explain them. For that latter type of stability, I would have to look elsewhere, assuming it could even be found. What Eliade gave me was a view of the world that could hold together during the search.

Eliade taught me that shamanism is a worldwide phenomenon. Although Eliade focuses on Siberian and Central Asian traditions and completely neglects Africa, he proves that shamanism has been practiced on every continent and, at one time or another, among most peoples. As with Buddhism, "religion" may not be an apt term with which to describe it. Everywhere, shamanism has been used for a similar constellation of social functions: communal and personal healing, divination, communication with the spirit world, and such services as escorting a dead person's spiritual residuum to the place where such entities reside. Despite variations attributable to cultural, environmental, and historical factors and influences, what shamanism consists of, both as practice and as social function, is broadly consistent throughout the world. The "Hawaiian" variety to which Samara introduced me would be recognizable and probably intelligible, at least in its essentials, to a Mongolian Buryat. A shaman Journeys by means of trance through realms more or less consistent with Samara's schematic description of the three Worlds. Certain symbols and activities are broadly common among these Worlds. Shamans typically are able to travel through them by a means identified as "flying." Commonly, the Worlds are connected to each other by a Tree or some such vertical structure—a mountain, a pole, a ladder. One way of moving among Worlds is to climb the Tree or to descend among its roots. I could go on. The list of commonalities is lengthy indeed. I've indicated only a few.

Leaving aside for the moment how we define "objective," my sense of the Garden's objective reality had been strongly corroborated. What I had encountered was not just an idiosyncratic fantasy generated within my head, peculiar to me. Shamans around the world, in the most various and disparate cultures, even cultures that had not interacted among each other, all had been experiencing and working with the same stuff. That is to say, what we were dealing with in shamanic trance was more or less basic to human perception and consciousness, a set of structures and features almost genetic in their universality and strongly individualized expression. The dreamworld's invisibility to persons living in modern societies was evidence of our blindness to it, not evidence of its unreality.

Eliade could not tell me whether shamanism's features and structures were purely artefacts of human mentation, reflecting only intracranial processes, or rather did they represent some type of interaction with perceptions of extra-cranial reality. Either way, I undeniably was dealing with something bigger than myself. This thought was comforting.

It bears repeating: shamans deal with something literally bigger than the individual. Eliade could not tell me how to distinguish with certainty between the aspects of any particular shaman's vocation that are socially constructed, that is, created by and/or for the social environment in which the shaman operates, on the one hand, and those aspects which are organic to that shaman's ability to access the dreamworld, on the other. Notwithstanding, the commonalities among shamanic experience of the dreamworld across cultures can mean only that even if you disregard what's socially conditioned, you are left with something irreducibly strange. Shamanism is fundamental to humanity, and humanity—not mere humans—is fundamental to shamanism. Allowing for a high degree of showmanship related to maintaining the traditional shaman's authority within the community, what remains is not mere fakery or hallucination. It is not just in their heads. Whether the explanation resides in the broad structures of human neurobiology, or in an objective reality not ordinarily accessible to the five senses, or in something other and perhaps even more exotic and difficult to articulate, shamans are and for thousands of years have been "on to something" that does not depend on what you and I as individuals believe.

It may be, as many but by no means all of Eliade's sources indicated, that the higher functions of shamanism, that is, healing, divination, the role of psychopomp, are not available to everybody. Not everybody can be a major league pitcher. Pretty nearly everybody, however, can learn to throw a baseball. Access to the shaman's view of reality appeared to be open to all. To say that this was an exploration I wanted to take "wherever and however far it might lead" would have been an exaggeration; but after reading Eliade, I was eager to pursue it a good ways further down the road. I wanted to be more in touch with the roots of my humanity, to know more of what it is to be human.

One thing that disappointed me about *Shamanism* was its lack of practical advice about how to be a shaman. Eliade indulges in a bit of speculation about the reasons that shamans prefer to work after dark or in dim places. Reading this, it struck me that Eliade not only had no anthropological fieldwork experience, he had no experience of trance.

In the last few decades, an increasing number of "how to" guides to trance have appeared in English. Perhaps foremost among them is *The Way of the Shaman* by Michael Harner, an anthropologist whose fieldwork had led him to become a shamanist practitioner and popularizer. He was one of the leading figures in the contemporary renaissance, if that is not too strong a term, of shamanism among the non-indigenous inhabitants of North America. Borrowing and synthesizing mostly Native American traditions, Harner has inspired and guided many. Closer to my own roots, I found *Magic of the Ordinary: Recovering the Shamanic in Judaism*, by Rabbi Gershon Winkler. Rabbi Winkler makes a fairly convincing case that the Torah, the Babylonian Talmud, and other Jewish writings preserve remnants of an ancient strain of shamanic nature-worship, which he thinks has been largely lost in the rabbinic era. From these shards, cobbled together with borrowings from Native Americans, Winkler has reconstructed a practice that works for him.

But Harner and Winkler left me cold. Their recommended procedures and rituals struck me as contrived, artificial. But they did point in a clear direction. Each had used found materials to construct programs that did work, and not only for them, if not for me.

Harner, Winkler, and the whole project of adapting indigenous knowledge to resurrect shamanistic practice in our culture, from which awareness of the dreamworld almost has died, necessarily confront the problem of how to use trance to access the dreamworld and to navigate among its entities and structures, when you don't possess a living tradition of doing so? Obviously, short of "re-inventing the wheel," one has to borrow from somewhere. This approach, necessitated by circumstance, was facilitated in modern North America by the history of re-engagement with shamanism through anthropological observation and scholarship in the history of religions.

In such a project, the potential for cultural appropriation inevitably is an issue. Harner skirts it by his explicitly synthetic, anthropologically based approach. Winkler takes the different tack of appealing to buried shamanistic strains in his own religious tradition, which he seeks to revive by grafting onto them elements of living, Native American traditions. By being honest and explicit about their borrowings from others' mental technologies and belief systems, properly attributing their source material without pretending any relationship with it to which they are not entitled, I felt that Harner and Winkler avoided cultural appropriation, even if sometimes just barely.

Of more practical usefulness to me, Harner, Winkler, and Eliade showed that there's no "one size fits all." I would cut my suit to my own pattern, from my own and borrowed cloth.

Thinking about Eliade, and Harner and Winkler and the rest, this poem came to me:

Somewhere within my ten fingers
I may find what makes myths move.
Joining hands in the sacred ring,
I cannot sing what the old ones sing.
My feet won't shuffle as theirs do.
Yet, the trembling palm-brush lingers.

16. February 8, 2021

Samara had been urging me to ascertain the nature, location, and condition of my Garden's boundaries. Although I already had visited the border at water's edge, this was only at one spot, so I had to admit that surveying the boundary was an uncompleted task. It seemed important to Samara that I do this, for reasons that remained obscure to me. I understood that having clear but appropriately permeable boundaries is an element of good psychological health. Maybe that was what it was about.

I drew the window shades on this sunny day, smudged with sage, then invoked the kindness and assistance of the six Directions, saluting each Direction with my shofar. I invoked the assistance of Mama Bear and her cubs, and of Badger. No Badger had thus far put in an appearance in the dream-world, but I had felt an affinity with badgers since childhood. Badger had been my favorite character in one of my favorite childhood books, Kenneth Graham's marvelous *Wind in the Willows*. If I had an animal alter ego, I wouldn't have minded for it to be a badger. It couldn't hurt to ask Badger's help.

I didn't use any formula of words. Instead, I spoke to each entity extemporaneously, reciting the qualities I associated with it: North, for example, being the Direction that pares things down to their bare core, the Direction of extremes, of harshness and the sudden, violent beauty of its spring, of long silence, of a brief, piercingly tender summer. I said that kind of thing. I surprised myself with how heartfelt this became.

Then I described the Journey's purpose of visiting the Garden, communicating with its inhabitants, and establishing its boundary. I lay down on the bed, started the drum music, and covered my eyes.

Almost immediately, I see trees. I am under a thick tree canopy, in the dark. Everything is black and white and slightly blurry, like a pinhole camera photograph. I greet the trees, "Hello, trees," but they do not respond. I am not in control of my motions. I glide among the trees at a walking pace. I glimpse a whitish something through them, a narrow path perhaps? Or is it the clearing where the farmhouse is?

I come to a place where my vision is not filled with trunks, branches, leaves, and needles. It is clearer, blanker. What am I looking at? It is a flat surface. Does it glimmer? It's water. It's the boundary. It's just like what I saw on that previous Journey to the border. My Garden is an island. Although I have seen the water at only these one or two spots, I just know this, as if something I had suspected has been confirmed by evidence. Indeed, before starting today's Journey, I'd thought that the Garden may be surrounded by water. Self-confirming prophecy? Perhaps, but the Garden has defied expectation nearly every time I've been here, so I am inclined to think not. The dreamworld doesn't seem to work that way. It's more as if the dreamworld were saying, "You wanted to see the boundary? Okay, here's the boundary. It's all like this. You don't need to see any more of it."

I go back under the trees and move through the woods. Now I am directing my movements. I come to the farmhouse. I ask, "Who are you? Why am I frightened of you?" It answers, "Come in." I do not hear the words as sounds, or see them as if written. They're just there. I see a door, already ajar. I hesitate, then enter.

Inside, it's dark as night, but I can tell I am moving through rooms with some furniture in them. There's a kitchen with a long counter, or breakfast bar, or island. There are stairs, upon which I am moving down to the basement and up to the next floor, both at the same time.

I am in an upstairs room, like an attic room, the bare, white walls closing to a peak above me. This must be in the short wing of the house. Here I see a small, white, rodent face. It looks straight at me, hints of pink in the ears and at the lips. It is a white rat. There are rats in the attic. I ask the house, "Who are you?" It says it's my childhood. I ask, "Why is it so dark in here?" The house answers, "Rats in the attic."

I go back downstairs. "How do I make a light in here?" I ask. "Find a light switch," says the house. "Where is that?" I ask, but the house doesn't answer. Looking around, I see several rectangular objects on the walls that might be light switches or electrical outlets, but nothing happens. I see a tiki torch leaning against a wall and think, maybe I could use that? But I don't even try. The thought of using it referred to a future time, not to the present moment.

I see white rats all over the house. They all are looking at me. They're neither scary nor repulsive. They seem curious about me, but none of them remains in sight long enough to talk to. A huge creature materializes, looming over me, sort of a cross between a carnivorous dinosaur like a tyrannosaurus or a velociraptor, and a praying mantis. It is a thoroughly fearsome creature, but I am not afraid of it. Like the rats, it disappears before I think to address any words to it.

The knowledge comes to me that it is time for me to get out of the house. Again, this is not a matter of fear. Fear of the house and the things in it is gone. It's just like closing time at the museum: the docent tells you to go, and you go. Only, there's no docent. I look for a door, but can't find one. I see trees through a sash window. I move towards it, with the thought of passing through it like a ghost passes through walls, but I find I can't do that. The laws of physics are capricious in this place. At this time, I'm not ghostly. I unlock the window, raise the lower pane, and climb out.

I'm under the trees, again. Everything is till monochromatic, black and white, dark, somewhat indistinct. I ask the trees, "Why is it so dark out here?" They say, "Because you're hurrying." So, I stop and just let the vision unfold and swirl and develop. I just watch. Gradually, I begin to see hints of color, mostly browns, at first, but shining like freshly washed hair. Gradually, I begin to see things in three dimensions, instead of the flat-on-a-movie-screen appearance they've had up until now. Overhead, I glimpse a blue, dawn sky, half obscured and mottled by puffy, dark grey clouds. For the first time in my Journeying, to my jubilation, my surroundings appear in the clarity and color and fully rounded solidity of "real" life or of a very vivid dream.

That instant, the drum calls me back to ordinary consciousness.

17. February 28, 2021

Samara continued to urge me to attend to my boundary. She had built a wall around her Garden, and seemed to think that I should do something similar. I kept forgetting to ask her why the boundary is so significant, whether to keep things out or keep things in or for some other reason. Reasons seemed less important, with regard to a place where you can walk both up and down stairs at the same time.

With the ritual I'd used on my last Journey, I felt I had developed a format that fit me personally, that worked well, and that I could sustain through repeated use. Improvisation on set themes within a flexible structural framework: that's jazz, it's Indian classical music. The latter analogue was particularly pertinent. I had loved listening to raga since my youth, when my mother had taken me to a Ravi Shankar concert. Often, it has put me into something resembling a trance state. One unforgettable time, I was sitting in the front row at a concert of the great Hindustani classical flautist Hariprasad Chaurasia. Towards the end of a particularly long raga, I resurfaced to the auditorium, opened my eyes, and discovered the tanpura player gazing fixedly at my nodding, swaying head. His eyes shifted when he caught me looking at him.

For this Journey, I stated the intention of walking the perimeter of my Garden, discovering what was there, and learning what, if anything, I should alter to make it more effective.

It begins as usual, looking up into tree branches' back-lit tracery. Although it is somewhat dark where I am, the images are sharply focused and well rounded, no longer the pinhole camera view. I'm on a pale path. I start to follow it through the woods.

Suddenly, a red light, like a sunset just before the horizon swallows it, washes over everything. After that, no longer in control of my movement, I glide steadily along as if carried by a current. I am puzzled by this, but not alarmed. I do not understand or recognize much of what I see. I have little idea where I am—well, no idea while it's happening, although, as the Journey ends, in retrospect it will seem clear enough. I ask several times, "Where am I?" but I get no response. I glimpse many things—vegetation, creatures, eyes looking at me, insects, fungi, rocks, fish (some with scary, toothy, open mouths)—but nothing stays in view long enough to recognize or intact with. It's not as if they fade away or scatter. Rather, I am swept past them.

A long time passing through a narrow, twisty tunnel, with rough, uneven walls, and often with a light variously bright or faint shining around a bend ahead of me. When I'm carried around the bend, the light dims or disappears. What is this tunnel? Am I going inadvertently to the Lower World? Am I being carried along by the current of a frozen-over stream, under the ice? I think it must be the latter.

I try to stop, with the idea that if I just stop moving, I'll get a steady view of where I am, but I can't stop. Where is it taking me?

I start to see blurry tree limbs, branches, and twigs in the direction of "up," not blurry as if through a pinhole camera but blurry as if looking up from underwater through the surface, or through a film of ice. I keep moving along at the same, steady rate.

I see, very clearly but fleetingly, closeup pebbles, evergreen twigs, mushrooms. It's become very foggy. Thick, white mists move among the things I'm looking at, concealing them almost as soon as I see them. I feel I have been ejected from the stream and am lying on my stomach, peering at what litters the bank just in front of my face. The stream has carried me in a counterclockwise direction, spewing me out on the bank outside my Garden.

18. July 9, 2021

Of all the elements in my Garden, the farmhouse had most insistently drawn me to itself. I felt that I would be evading something essential, if I were to avoid returning there. I had to go back to the house, communicate with the rats, get the lights on, find out why the lights were out in the first place. Had the rats nibbled away the wiring? Read those last two sentences one way, and they sound goofy, or even silly. But the images carried weight, and that weight gave me pause. What did all this signify, in terms of the life I believed I had been leading? It was one thing to talk about property damage caused by cute little white rats. It was another thing altogether, to deal with the idea that "the house of my childhood" had "gone dark."

I was in the process of accepting trance as a source of meaningful perspective and information about myself. Rapidly, I had come a long way from mere curiosity and thrill seeking, and from intellectual curiosity about "structures of consciousness."

Considered as figures of speech, as metaphors, "house of childhood" and "darkening" could be interpreted many ways. So, for that matter, could "rats." I suspected many things. What adult doesn't find it difficult to remember childhood, as it was? Who hasn't experienced some trauma along the way, that might have "darkened" it? Who has not lost some part of themselves to the thousand corrosive, relentless bites of error, time, and circumstance? I suspected that my Journeys implicated such things. And it was one thing to consider such ideas in the abstract, but now they had become very personal.

It was too much weight for me to carry into the unknown all at once. If I say, I needed time to get used to it, that is probably an accurate statement of what went on over the next four months, but it misleadingly suggests that it was a consciously considered process. It says nothing about my actual state of mind. I knew that my next Journey would take me to the house. I knew that I could not go there until I was ready. I knew that I would know that I was ready, when I was ready. Meanwhile, I chewed over and over the theories, potential implications, suppositions, ramifications, and barely acknowledged trepidations suggested by the darkened house, the rats, the giant predatory lizard/insect. The cumulative weight of these speculations only made me procrastinate more.

At last, overcoming whatever may have constituted this inner resistance, or perhaps because the resistance had spun itself out to the point of exhaustion, I announced my intention to go to my Garden to talk with the rats in the House of my childhood.

Treetops, sky. The sky is bright grey, overcast with round clouds packed together like cobblestones.

Abruptly, I am in darkness. I wonder where I am. I become certain that I am in the House. I see miscellaneous, disconnected details of rooms—a corner, a windowsill. I look for the rats. I conduct a careful, lengthy inspection of long, taped drywall joint, which I think may be the peak of the attic ceiling, looking for rodent holes.

I keep thinking I am about to see a rat, but I don't. Last time I was here, they were everywhere. "Come to me, rats. I won't hurt you. I mean you no harm. I want to talk with you." Silence. Where are the rats, I wonder.

I enter the cavities within the walls. Maybe I pass ghost-like through drywall, or maybe I squeeze into the end of a partition at an opening where the sheetrock was left off or removed, or maybe I do both. I have a stronger visual image of the latter. Although I have no memory of entering through such a gap, I saw one shortly before I found myself within the wall. I am thinking, the rats would be in the walls.

If it was dark before, it's even darker in here. The darkness is broken here and there by faint glimmers of color, or dust reflecting rays of what little light has seeped from the dimness outside the wall through cracks or holes. I glimpse portions of objects I can't see enough of to recognize.

A big, black wasp is sitting in front of me. It's as big as I am. I can't see its head or wings, but the position of its abdomen indicates the head is towards me. Why is it here? Maybe to help me? "Wasp, will you take me to the rats?" No answer. I remember that wasps are parasitic. Maybe this one wants to lead me astray, to use me for its own purposes. Maybe I shouldn't trust it.

A furry, whiskered, grey and black face appears, looking at me. It is Badger. The wasp is gone. Has Badger made the wasp go away? "Badger, help me find the rats." But Badger, if that's who it was, disappears. "Rats, I want to talk with you."

I wander more within the walls. Hard to tell up from down, but I do go up, towards the attic. Up, ahead of me, is a very old, wooden door. Its brown wood is covered with what could be an elaborate pattern of intricate carvings, or maybe it's just the feathery whiskers of old, dried-out, weathered wood, or both. The door is closed. Are the rats through there? It takes a while, but I manage to get through the door without actually opening it. Nothing is on the other side.

At some point, maybe this point, I leave the House through a window. Once outside, I am facing the woods, but I turn around. "I want to see the House from outside," I say. It is no longer the plain, old, ell-shaped farmhouse. It is a big Victorian, with several wings, gables, round turrets, a captain's walk.

I go back in. I see multiple visions of a window that has some sort of vertical object in front of it, perhaps a candlestick. I know that this window was significant to my childhood, but I don't know what the significance is, and I do not think to ask. Nor do I think to light the candlestick.

I ask, "House, where are the rats?"

The House answers, "They're not here. They're gone."

"Where are they gone to?"

"Dust."

"Can I find the dust?"

No answer. I imagine taking a pinch of the dust between thumb and forefinger. It is a very fine, grey powder, like marijuana ash. I ask, "Can I turn on the lights?"

"No," says the House.

"How can I know you better?"

"You must live in me."

"How can I do that?"

"Light a fire in the hearth."

"Show me the hearth."

After a while, I see the hearth. I see it multiple times,

from multiple angles. First, it is dark and cold. Then bright, red filaments arc across it, like the hairs that are emblematic of the fox, only it is not the fox. Then there are coals in the hearth, round charcoal briquettes, packed together like the clouds I saw at the beginning of the Journey, red glowing from the bottom layer through the interstices of the top layer, which has not yet ignited fully. Without consciously intending to, I have lit the hearth. At that moment, the Journey ends.

19.

I had changed the Garden. Although at no point had I said explicitly, "I am going to light the hearth," the act was unquestionably volitional. I'd done it as a matter of course once I learned that I had to in order to achieve a more intimate relationship with the House and all it represented. I'd known I was going to light the hearth at least as soon as I'd seen it. What troubled me now was that contrary to Samara's warnings I hadn't investigated what it would mean to do so, and what the consequences might be. But if Samara was right, it would change my life.

A year and four months earlier, on March 19, 2020, almost precisely at the conjunction of covid's arrival in my home state of Vermont and Samara's request for help with her homework, I had finished work on the final volume of *In Dante's Wake*, a trilogy of narrative poems.[6] It had been a seventeen years' labor of love. Almost every day, except for an interval after each book was done, I had worked on

6 *In Dante's Wake* consists of *To Join the Lost* (Antrim House 2010, reissued by Fomite Press 2016), *Among the Lost* (Fomite Press 2016, and *Once Was Lost* (Fomite Press 2021).

this project, even if it was only to set down a single line or a revision of a line; not a day had gone by without giving considerable thought to it.

I had anticipated a fallow period, a time of regeneration, to follow the trilogy's completion. After finishing each of the first two volumes, months had passed before I resumed writing verse. My inspiration had been spent; the well was dry; the battery needed recharging. These were the terms I used to explain it to myself. Those months had been uncomfortable for me, times of frustrated creativity, alleviated only by confidence that I would begin the next book when the battery once again could spark, when the well once again brimmed with water. All I had to do was wait, let nature take its course, be open to whatever life may show me, and exercise patience, difficult as that last may be.

This third time had been different. No next book beckoned me into the future, no clear idea what my next project may be, no certainty whether there was to be a next project at all. Very little prose and not even occasional poems came to me. The Muse was mute. I had told myself, you've just finished a seventeen-year, all-consuming project, you're going to need a lot of time to readjust. Meanwhile, I had said to myself, you have other creative outlets. You like to build furniture. You like to garden. You're learning to make things on a lathe. Do those.

But my identity, centered on the writing of poetry, had begun to waver. A poet who has no poetic output to show for a long enough period, at some point becomes an ex-poet. The phrase "shot my wad" had been coming to mind uncomfortably often, and with it an inner feeling of emptiness and dryness.

Okay, I had told myself, maybe I could resign myself to that. This wouldn't have been the first time I'd been through a major transition like this. In 2017, I'd retired from a thirty-two years long legal career. But with the completion of *In Dante's Wake*, unlike with the mere transition to retirement from a more-or-less satisfying livelihood, the work that I had thought was my true work, the purpose that I had thought was mine, had vanished. I had no idea how to recover them, and nothing in sight that might take their place. All I could see on the horizon was a threatening boredom.

Then, in July 2021, I rekindled the hearth.

About a month later, another loss occurred. After a long illness, my cat died. She'd been born in the Vermont town of Montgomery, so when my then-wife had brought the kitten home, it was an obvious choice for us, both fans of John Prine, to name her Angel. She had lived with me most of her twenty years, coming with me to my new home when my marriage failed. Angel was a strong, quirky personality. I loved her. The last several years, she had been afflicted with progressive, untreatable kidney failure. Her decline had been so slow as to be imperceptible until mid-August, when it became precipitous. She was wasting away. At last, to spare her unnecessary suffering, I took her in for euthanization. It was not a difficult decision, but it was a painful one.

Almost immediately upon Angel's demise, I began to write again: copiously, fluently; perhaps even, at first, too copiously and fluently, almost obsessively. The battery surged, nearly overheated. The well overflowed. Within weeks, I produced a 9,655 word essay about Angel, our life together, and her passing.

Less than two months after that, I realized that this book was my next project. I felt I had regained my mojo.

I wrote the following poem in 1997. Its resonance with the events I've described above is emotional, rather than discursive. It was written shortly after the death of my father. The poem refers to that, and conflates the births of my children in 1988 and 1991 into a single event. It is included here, at this place in this book, because that is what it demanded of me:

Low Light

I have beheld the end of a life,
blue eyes turning to the ceiling
and closing, and the strange, orange hue
that then suffused the cooling skin,

and a life's beginning I've also beheld,
the mewling, stick-limbed lump of tenderness,
eyes clamped shut, trading the womb
for its exhausted mother's arms.

It's odd to hold them both within me,
pale lights at each end of a stick.
They do not balance: the one cannot be
weighed with the other or cancel it out.

Some console themselves with rhythms,
tell the children the gracefully falling
leaves make mulch for what will rise,
as if the steady beat of days, of

seasons, generations, and decay
drowns the silence. Others, by droning
of the eternal, attempt to flood it.
In the body's sealed envelope, we

carry to the inarticulate young
from lips forever shrunken open
a sediment of sentiment.
It gives them heft to bear their growth.

Devoted as robins to their hatchlings,
we pass it down the straining gullet;
unlike them, we're no more empty
for giving our young what we had in us.

Passing on is not unburdening.
When my father died, he handed me
a weight no one could bring into
this world except by leaving it.

My children bleated their little welcomes
in that same building's other wing.

20. Halloween 2021

The festival of Spirits seemed a propitious date upon which to launch into consolidating my relationship with the Garden, further exploring it and meeting new inhabitants, developing my Journeying skills, and preparing to venture into the Lower World. In the spirit of starting by tying up loose ends, I announced my intention to cross the Garden and talk with the lollipop-shaped tree and whatever other entities I may encounter.

It's never what was expected.

At this Journey's end, I felt that it had been the most chaotic thus far, a kaleidoscopic mishmash. I could make sense of almost none of it. I had only a rare and intermittent sense of being in the Garden. Not infrequently, the Journey seemed to be on the verge of coalescing into intelligibility, but it never quite got there. I never was sure what was happening, or where I was. Afterwards, I could not write about this Journey in the present tense, that is, as though I were inside it.

Only three things occurred that stuck in memory. The first may have been an example of the way that things encountered in one Journey so often reappear in another, in more developed form. I was feeling pretty strongly on the verge of seeing something stable enough to recognize. The idea occurred to me of helping it along by humming. An odd, groaning, modal tune emerged from my throat. I wasn't consciously shaping the sounds, just letting them happen. The tune evolved into something like a hummed yodel. My skin tingled. The treetop that I thought might be forming out of the chaos, emerging to stand out against a bright sky, began to develop a spring greenish hue. The brightness grew brighter. The feeling strengthened that the Something was about to happen; also, that things might go out of control. My humming became self-conscious, performative. I stopped doing it. Whatever had been emerging out of the chaos, fell back into it.

Soon after that, I attempted to converse with the tree that I had intended to visit, on the assumption that even if I couldn't see it or sense its presence it might be there anyway, but that did not go well. I asked the tree what it represented, and the reply came back a bit too quickly. "Toenail fungus." Something told me that it could be treated with tea tree oil. (In the "real" world, I'd had toenail fungus, and had treated it successfully with tea tree oil.)

At last, not long before the drum called me back, I perceived myself flying above the clouds in the company of several bats. It was unclear to me whether I was riding on a bat or flying on my own. At least bats seemed appropriate to the occasion.

The next day, November 1, in a state of doubt and discouragement, I typed the above paragraphs from the notes I scribble after every Journey. I was sitting at my dining room table, sun flooding over the yew hedge outside and through the bay window on my right. Suddenly, a squirrel leaped out of the hedge. It scrabbled against the window as if to dig its way through. A few minutes later, a bird banged into the window, making a low, ringing sound. It bounced back atop the hedge and sat there for a little while, recovering its wits, before flying away.

I wrote this poem in 1978, to go on a Halloween party invitation:

Halloween 1978

O cover me clothing against the night
for that wild naked dance I so love
whirls ever higher twirling to shatter
what day holds dear with one slender kick
O sheath that holds my form inviolate
O simple restraint
so easily slashed
flutter on the talon's tip
I await my Word to be free

21. November 10, 2021

In the spirit (lower case "s") of "git back on the horse what threw ya," I stated my intention for this day's Journey as being "to visit my Garden and see what's there."

I start by trying to visualize the bell of my shofar, to use it as a portal to the Middle World, but nothing doing. It just won't appear. Apparently, my Journeys don't work that way. I don't need a portal. I just go there.

Instead of the expected treetops, it begins with rays of white light emanating in a starburst pattern through sheer, pitch blackness. I watch it for a while, until I stop expecting the treetops to appear. Then I watch the radiant pinpoint a while longer.

Blackness, deep and velvety. An animal face appears out of it, looking at me head on; fades; reappears; fades and reappears multiple times. Thinking I recognize it, I ask, "Are you Badger?"

"Yes." The voice, although not an auditory phenomenon, is pitched low and soft.

I ask, "Where are we?"

The answer is ambiguous. I am not sure whether Badger says "a tunnel" or "my burrow." Maybe both.

I ask Badger, "Where are you taking me? Where are we going?"

"To the Lower World."

I say, "Okay, let's go to the Lower World."

I follow Badger. The tunnel is very long, twisty, and dark. I smell a dry smell, maybe the sage I smudged with in preparation for the Journey, but somewhat staler than that. Maybe an animal smell—Badger? Now and again,

I see glimmers of blue light, electric blue like a cop car's flashers. Sometimes I feel the tunnel open wider around me and I'm in a spacious chamber; then it narrows again; then it opens, perhaps even wider than before, into an airy cavern; then it narrows to a passage not much larger than my body.

I say to Badger, "Teach me. I follow you." A song comes to me. It consists of three longer notes, a short note, and a short rest. The second note is half a step higher than the first and third notes. The fourth, short note is lower than them. I feel that Badger is teaching me this song. I don't know what it's for. He doesn't say, and I don't ask. I sing it repeatedly. Although the song has a very simple rhythm, which might be written as three half notes followed by a quarter note and a quarter rest, it keeps creeping out of sync with the metronomic drum beat underlying the Journey. I have some concern at first that I might be distracted out of my trance by using my body like this, but the song doesn't seem to have any effect on my experience as we move through the tunnel. After a while, the song moves from my chest up my throat and into my nose. I begin to feel as if my singing is becoming merely performative. At that point, it seems like it's time to stop singing, so I do.

The tunnel continues—long, twisty, and dark. I worry sometimes that Badger is not with me anymore, that I may have fallen too far behind. I call to him, usually some variation of "Teach me, Badger. I follow you." In response, I receive the sense that he is here, not very far ahead of me in the blackness. Sometimes I see flares of colorless light. I can't identify any source for them. It's like a very bright flashlight reflecting off a crystal. Sometimes I dimly perceive shapes around me. There's the smooth, glossy, blue-black, chitinous abdomen of a large insect, an ant or a spider perhaps, or a wasp; moss and tree roots hang from the ceiling, brushing me as I pass beneath them; mineral icicles. Interspersed among these, since the early part of the Journey, I see red faces with big, square, red teeth, like Mayan masks, that emerge out of the darkness and almost immediately disappear, each time sparking a brief frisson of fear.

At long, long last, there's a faint glow ahead of me that persists as I approach it. It looks like twilight filtering through a window of many clear glass panes, cut and leaded so as to make a picture. The window entirely extends across the tunnel's end, side to side and up and down. It could be a gate. Its heavy leading and many, variously shaped panes depict a human brain, a side view, showing in outline the gyres and sulci, the cortical folds. I ask, "Is that the Lower World?" I mean what lies beyond the window. "Yes," says Badger.

And at that moment the drum ends the Journey.

22.

As we had done each month since the early covid shutdowns, Samara and I took our takeout cartons of breakfast sandwiches and pastries to the deserted State Office Building in Waterbury, Vermont, there to sip coffee, munch goodies, talk, and laugh. I valued these meetings now more than ever, not only for Samara's always entertaining friendship, but for the relief they provided from confusion and isolation. It was a time of confusion and isolation for the whole world, of course, as we all groped for ways to cope with the new and all too often deadly virus. At the same time, for me, even greater confusion arose from the new and strange reality opened up through Journeying, that I increasingly felt it was important to explore. The isolation that most affected me at this time was due to the difficulty, the near impossibility really, of sharing meaningful conversation about the dreamworld with anyone who had not been there. Learning to practice "social distancing" as a prophylactic against infection paled in comparison. That was something easily palliated by contact through a mask or online or (most precious) with one's trusted "pod" of friends and family. It did not come close to matching the isolation of having next to no one to talk with about profound and troubling experiences.

For two and a half hours this November 14, not an unusual duration for our get-togethers, the conversation ranged widely but spared plenty of time for shamanism. I told Samara about my tendency to blurred vision while Journeying, as if seeing things through a pinhole camera or badly focused lens. I shared my theory that this had something to do with the right hemisphere of the brain's preferential processing of longer-frequency light-waves. I was, at this time, deep into a quest to ground my shamanic trance experiences in neuroscience. It constituted an almost desperate effort on my part to bring the dreamworld into the realm of reality that I already recognized, and thereby to limit and control it, to stabilize the shifting sands I stood on without having to give up too much of what was familiar or to go further beyond the familiar than was comfortable. But it was a fascinating study in its own right, despite the paucity of neuroscientific research directly bearing on these issues.

Samara reminded me that the basic lesson for me at this early stage of my education was to relax control over the Journey, to get my mind out of the way of what was happening, to open to the experience, and to let it flow. I remembered how prescriptive I had been in declaring my intention for the "failed," chaotic trip, and how, suspecting I had been overly controlling, I had announced a much looser purpose for the most recent Journey, during which I had met Badger, learned a song, and seen things clearly. "There's no such thing as a failed Journey," said Samara. Every one presents you with something to learn from. She concurred that I might be impairing my experience by trying too much to direct it, by not allowing it to unfold in all its expansiveness. Playing with the pinhole simile, she said, "You're trying to squeeze it through this tiny, . . ."

I had been thinking too much! It was not much of a revelation that I might overthink things, but it struck me forcefully enough that I almost forgot to tell Samara about something I had come across in a book[7] I was reading two days after meeting Badger: Malaysian shamans learn songs from their Spirit Animal Helpers one phrase at a time!

We agreed that Journeys have a funny manner of strictly and literally obeying the announced intention for them, but

7 Graham Harvey, editor, *Shamanism: a reader* (Routledge 2003)

of doing so in quirky and unpredictable ways. For example, my most recent Journey's purpose "to visit my Garden and see what's there." And it stayed in the Garden, literally in the ground beneath, while the Spirit who had appeared to guide me, Badger, clearly meant to direct my attention to the pathway through the Garden's subterranean features to the Lower World. He'd taken me right up to the Lower World's gates, leaving not a second to go beyond them. (Another way of interpreting the imagery was that the passage to the Lower World had been barred by my brain.) Samara emphasized that it is important to be very careful when setting a Journey's purpose. She gave me guidelines to being sufficiently specific but not too restrictive. First, I must state a destination. Second, I should pose a query to which, upon arriving at the destination, I hoped to find an answer. Upon arrival, or even on the way, there would be many entities with whom I might communicate.

Preoccupied with the difficulty of communicating about the dreamworld, I expressed discomfort with referring to its inhabitants as "Spirits." I explained my feeling that the word invites misunderstanding. In our culture, "spirits" refers to a specific if broad set of connotations and associations: but we're not talking about Casper the Friendly Ghost here. Traditional shamans may use words which can be translated as "spirit," but such a translation forgets that the shaman is using a technical vocabulary developed in the shaman's culture which has no exact counterpart in a culture from which shamanism is largely absent. I said I liked the phrase "other-than-human persons" used in Graham Harvey's book. His locution struck me as unwieldy, but perhaps more accurate, unless the entities we're talking about are in the end nothing more than aspects of the shamanic traveler's psyche. In that case, I said, I had no idea what to call them.

Samara, who, unlike me, had more than one friend with whom she could talk about these matters, didn't respond directly. Staying within her role of mentor, she said that different types of "other-than-human person" might have different types of information for me. From entities encountered as features or inhabitants of the "places" to which I might Journey, I could get information of a symbolic nature. For example, the "lights are out" in the "house" that is my "childhood" but I may "learn to live there" by "lighting the hearth." Spirits acting as guides such as Badger might explain this symbolism in language more accessible to conventional consciousness, and might teach me what actions might be indicated for me to take.

So far, I hadn't even thought of asking a guide for that kind of help. I had just met Badger! Perhaps such interaction awaited me in the Lower World, where, Samara said, ancestral guides awaited me.

Later, thinking about my well-nigh unbreakable habit of overthinking everything, this poem came to me:

Lay down the crude tools
you torture the earth with
take a deep breath
eat a sandwich
brew a nice cup of tea
pick up the phone
and call your mother

23. November 18, 2021

I wanted to see if I could go deeper into the dreamworld more easily with music other than the boomboomboom of traditional shamanic drumming. I knew from reading Eliade and other anthropological sources that drums are only one of many means that shamans use to drown out external audible stimuli, deaden responses to them, and evoke the trance state. I had begun to worry that I was listening to the drum too much. Although the drumming is extremely monotonous, I had found myself detecting tunes in the tones and the overtones of its resonance, meandering above and in and out of the drone. My compulsion to "do it right" (which, after all, had served me quite well in my legal career) made me concerned that I shouldn't be doing this, that I was somehow distracting myself from something I should be doing or paying attention to instead. Maybe another music wouldn't incur these problems. Think think think.

On Wendy Halley's web site, I had found a recording that sounded rather like one of those "Guatemalan rainfall" white noise tracks. After about ten seconds of that, I already felt spacey. I decided to try it on my next Journey. The previous Journey had plunked me down in a passage to the Lower World. Now, I wanted to find out where that passage's entrance is located in my Garden, follow it all the way to the end, and "look around."

Throughout this Journey, I am continuously aware to varying degrees of my body lying on my bed, my gentle breathing, the air in my nostrils, such transitory physical sensations as an itch in my left eyelid. The electronic soundtrack carries me along, but I never sink into it, unlike the drum. At some point on nearly every Journey with the drum, I leave the ordinary world far enough behind that I'm no longer conscious of it.

Nevertheless, I do reach the Garden. I look up into the usual treetops and the bright sky behind them. The sight comes in short bursts, never taking up my whole field of vision. I see something like sparse grass stalks on top of a mound. It reminds me of the burrow/mound I saw so long ago on one of my first Journeys. I remember I had suspected at that time that it may contain a passage to the Lower World. I smell briefly that sweet/dry scent, a bit musky, a bit like sage, that I have begun to associate with Badger. Or maybe it's just the smudge.

Then all is velvety blackness, in which I see a glimmer like a pinpoint light on ice. Things flare into view and disappear. This is not like the tunnel I was in with Badger, however. There is no sense of a physical space containing me.

At this point, another feature of this Journey rises to the foreground and remains there until the end: uncertainty. I am unsure where I am, what is happening, what I am seeing, who if anyone I am dealing with. Mushrooms appear and fade into the darkness. One, at least, has a red cap with white dots: amanita muscaria? I feel alone. But then there are hints of presences. An animal's eye close to my face inspects me, half of an animal's face becomes visible around it, with a long muzzle—not badger-like markings—is it Mama Bear?

A face like a human skull flares out of the darkness, fades, returns with its mouth wide open, its eye sockets turned upwards. It looks as if it might be screaming, but there's no sound. I ask who it is. There's no direct reply, but I have an uncertain sense, for no reason that I could name, that it is my long-dead maternal grandmother.

I don't know whether I have reached the Lower World yet, because according to things I've read, which I think I probably take too literally and place too much weight on, I should see light when I get there, and I don't. I wonder whether the passage to the Lower World is a place one might expect to meet an ancestor. Again, according to things I've read one can meet the dead in the Garden, in the Middle World. Is the passage from the Middle to the Lower World a part of the former? Think think think.

My cognition becomes slow, sluggish. The question forms, do you love me? Do you love me? It feels as if the question is coming from me, and as if it is a question I have for her, that is, my grandmother, but at the same time it does not feel as if I am the one who is asking it. There is no answer.

A burst of bright, blue-green-white light reveals a human figure, surrounded by the light, leaning over far to her right. I can't see her body because it is draped head to toe in robes, but I know, in a rare moment of certainty, that it is the woman whom I identified as my grandmother. Then she's gone.

The question repeats, do you love me? This time it is my question, although I haven't consciously intended or formed it.

She appears again, this time in more normal, daylight illumination. The robes covering her are very thick, coarse, brown cloth. She rolls over on top of me. I feel her body on top of mine. It is not exactly a physical sensation, not the burden and contours of an adult, female human. Rather, there is an access of weight on me, a definite but immeasurable pressure. I think, she is hugging me. Then, she disappears and the darkness returns.

I linger in the darkness for a while. I keep expecting light to dispel it, to show me where I am, but it doesn't. I feel presences all around me, hidden. At neither this, nor at any other time during the Journey, am I frightened.

Despite the Journey's dramatic events, I emerged from it feeling initially dissatisfied, as if nothing much had happened, as if the trance had not been deep enough. I had an urge to repeat the trip almost immediately, to go back and try to get more. Only when actually writing my notes did I realize how much had occurred.

Later, with more experience, I would come to recognize this as a not infrequent set of reactions to a Journey. At the time, I blamed it on the music. I thought (*think think think*) that the rain stick drone had not carried me deep enough, hence the uncertainty, continuing dual awareness of trance and ordinary reality, and delayed recollection. I decided to go back to the drum.

24.

In retrospect, the November 18 Journey marked the point at which I began to invest progressively diminishing attention in such things as neuroscientific investigation. It just seemed less and less relevant to the importance of what was happening. Already, my sojourns in the dreamworld arguably had produced one major impact on my life. After lighting the hearth, I was writing again and in full possession of my identity as a poet. But it could be argued equally persuasively that such a change was due to happen anyway; it could have been merely coincidental that the dam burst shortly after I changed the Garden. Now, however, with my grandmother, the whole thing had become intensely personal in an entirely different way. In a contest between personal significance and neurological speculations, personal significance wins every time.

My maternal grandmother had died over 45 years before. Learning that, the question uppermost in your mind, dear reader, may be, "Do you believe that the Journey brought you into contact with your dead grandmother?" It certainly was among the questions uppermost in my mind! Despite the implausibility of any such thing, the more I contemplated it the less I felt I had a simple, "yes or no" answer.

Another way of asking that question is, was the robed woman who hugged me a resident of my head, that is, with no existence apart from the neurological activity contained within my skull; or was she an image presented to me as the result of my brain processing data that it had received from sources ultimately outside my body? Of these two alternatives—figment of my mentation or independent, autonomous "Spirit"—it seemed to me that, even if Occam's Razor sliced away the latter, I still lacked proof as to the former. My dabblings in neuroscience had provided some starting points, but no conclusion.

I thought of it this way: a person's brain assembles an understanding of another person from sense data, memories, empathetic inferences, and other information about them of which we may not have been consciously aware while it was being compiled. The subject's status vis-à-vis breathing is pretty much irrelevant to their representation as a distinct personality accessible to us within consciousness. That representation can be very detailed and vivid. We may even believe with good reason that we know what grandma would say, what she would do, how she would look, if she were here. Sometimes, this rises to an almost sensual level. We may "hear" what she would say about something, in her own voice. The knowledge at the basis of these representations exists in the form of constellations of our own neurons communicating among themselves with chemicals and electricity. In short, to the extent that we observed, remembered, and captured an understanding of that other personality, it has become a physically active part of us. Would it not be meaningful, then, to say that my grandmother's "Spirit" lives on in my neurobiology? Sure, that Spirit would be shaped (so to speak) by my own biases, perceptual flaws, and ignorance, but would it not of necessity possess a core of objective truth? After all, I did not originate the data from which the Spirit was derived. This Spirit was grounded (so to speak) in my grandmother's own life history, an existence entirely external to my own. In her own lifetime, at least, she had not been a hallucination. And I was not the only person left in possession of a residue left by that existence. In the Venn diagram that may be drawn from those circles of residue, what is contained in the area where they intersect?

Oh, that word "possession!" It had scary overtones, which could not be avoided. My Journey had included more than a hint of possession. What would it mean to be possessed by an entity that exists as part of your physical being to begin with? Is the answer to that question the same, regardless how many circles there are in the Venn diagram, and regardless whether any of them intersect with yours? Is it relevant that my Journey only flirted with possession, that even at the moments when our identities had seemed to blur so much that I couldn't tell who was speaking, I continued to feel strongly the alterity of the entity I was dealing with? How does that add up? Who possessed whom, and when?

Or maybe this was the really important question: whether

there was any continuity between my grandmother's experience of herself when she was alive in her own right, on the one hand, and the experience of the entity represented to me as her during my Journey, on the other? But to ask that question, I had to assume that the word "entity" may be applied appropriately to whatever "she" was, and to assume further that, if so, said entity was capable of something that properly may be described as "experience" in the same sense as I would use that word regarding my mother's mother. What does "continuity" mean, in this context? And didn't those assumptions just bring me back, full circle, to the quandary I started with? Was there continuity between her experience of herself external to me, and whatever experiences may have occurred for my biologically internalized version of her?

Having led you into the tangle of knots that my mind was so busily tying around itself, I now leave you there, smack dab in the middle of the maze, as it were; because, frantic as all this cogitation was, it was of very secondary importance to me. Although I masticated thoroughly all these issues of evidence, reality, and identity, with each chew I cared a little less what the answers might be, or even whether there are answers. It just didn't seem to matter.

My relationship to my maternal grandmother during her lifetime had been deeply perturbed. The question "Do you love me?" would have been both completely appropriate and completely unlikely for either of us to have spoken during her lifetime. Long after her death, long before my involvement with shamanic trance, the relationship had been the subject of extensive and fruitful exploration with a therapist, the outcome being that I had considered all major issues related to it as fully resolved, the unspoken question notwithstanding. Indeed, in light of the resolution we had achieved, my therapist and I, the unspoken question was irrelevant. For my grandmother to return to me now, in this manner, was profoundly startling.

Thinking about the Journey the day after it occurred, sadness welled up in me and condensed in my tear ducts. That night, after I went to bed, before sleeping, I spoke aloud unpremeditated words of love and forgiveness. They came from no one's heart but mine. It felt like returning an unexpected and unexpectedly welcome hug. The next day this poem came to me:

Grandma in Flight

troubled awkward and quiet
trusting all these years
to hold who you were

just as one of hundreds
seated in a winged tube
(somewhere in the rear
a baby cries) trusts
without thinking it will
hold the air

longer than a breath and
touching down someone
at the gate will find and
breathlessly greet you

25.

As it is said, when the student is ready, the teacher appears. Samara sent me a link to Wendy Halley's podcasts.[8] Preoccupied with recovering my equilibrium, so shaken by the impact of November 18, I let the link sit in my inbox for a few weeks. Finally, in an impulsive, idle moment, I clicked on it.

From the three podcasts I listened to over the next few days, I learned perhaps more about Samara's teacher than I did about shamanism. Unlike the far out woo-woo New Agery that I had feared, Halley presented herself as a no-nonsense, level-headed, thoughtful, intelligent, rational person, passionate and knowledgeable about her work, but also endowed with a healthy level of humility in the face of the mysteries implicit in it. She seemed refreshingly and reassuringly free of the cheap, easy "mysticism" and "spirituality" that one so often encounters among persons purporting to retail ancient, indigenous wisdoms. In short, she talked in a way that I could understand and relate to.

Wendy showed no signs of hucksterism, she appeared to be the real deal, whatever "real" may mean in this context. In one of the podcasts, she talked about her introduction to shamanism. Several decades ago, about the time that she had become a licensed psychotherapist, she had undergone several spontaneous, visionary experiences, including a dream in which a strange man forcefully fed her knowledge. She never had seen or met him in waking life. Sometime later, she had encountered him at a conference. He was Hank Wesselman, Ph.D., an anthropologist, one of the early pioneers of the

8 https://www.lucidpathwellness.com/lucid-cafe-podcast

contemporary shamanist revival in Western society. Like several others of his generation of anthropologists, he had decided that maybe these shamans they were encountering in their fieldwork might be onto something worth studying on its own terms, in its own right. Moreover, he'd possessed the courage to act accordingly, even at the considerable professional risk of being accused by less enlightened colleagues—which is to say, most of them—of abandoning his status as an objective, scholarly observer and, in the demeaning vernacular phrase in which such accusations might be bandied, of "going native." Wesselman had trained Halley in the Hawaiian traditions from which he had learned.

I emailed Wendy:

> Hello, Wendy. I'm a friend and former colleague of Samara Anderson. I think she has talked to you about me. A while ago I helped Samara out with a homework assignment you gave her—find someone's power animal—and this evolved into Samara guiding me into my own shamanic practice. I'm using your excellent workbook. I'll get this out of the way right off—it has been an incredibly fascinatinag and powerful experience so far, and I'm just at the very beginning of it. I do not think that my path lies primarily in the direction of healing, except as it incidentally involves healing myself; but, traditionally, shamans had many other functions in the community besides that of healer. Healer may be the one that fits best into the very limited space allowed for shamanic practice in our society, but there are other paths. As Samara may have told you, in addition to being a former lawyer, I am a poet and a woodworker. (There's a point to all this. I'm getting to it.) It feels to me that the purpose of my exploration of shamanism

> is that I want to hear what the world is telling me, and insofar as the message is not meant for me alone, I want to find language or other means to pass it along. This is something I believe that traditional shamans do/did. So (finally coming to the point) although I know your practice is located in healing, I wonder whether you might be able to coach me, to help me on what appears to be this other path. I know efficiency and goal-directedness are very far from what shamanic practice is about, to say the least, but I feel a need for help in finding my way into what I am doing. I can flounder along on my own, but maybe I can get deeper faster with more teaching. Samara tells me that you do this kind of coaching. Would you be willing to take me on?

Two days later, apologizing unnecessarily for her tardiness, Wendy replied:

> I'm really happy to hear that you're exploring a shamanic path for yourself. It sounds like you're discovering how rich this territory can be. I agree that shamans have traditionally played many roles—not just the role of healer. I know practitioners who focus on working with plant medicines, facilitating rituals and ceremonies, have a psychopomp focus, etc. Lots of different ways to work with the unseen realms, which is exciting. In my practice I work with shamanism a few ways—primarily doing healing work, some ceremonial work (weddings and funerals) and house/property clearings. But an area I'm really excited about, which is what Samara referenced, is helping folks develop their own personal shamanic practice (which is why I created the workbook). That being said, I'd be happy to work with you in that capacity.

At Wendy Halley's web site, I booked an hour and a half training session for the latter part of January.

This poem came to me while I was writing this section:

knobby branches rapping
at the window skritching
let me in let me in

all night in the morning
they're not there there's nothing
on the pane but clear sky

26. December 8, 2021

The dreamworld seemed to have a mind of its own, and it seemed to be directing me into the Lower World. Although I had not been following the workbook precisely, I had reached the stage at which it, too, would have me go there. I picked the workbook exercise that seemed most relevant. It was to go to the Lower World and find my "Guardian Animal Spirit."

Unlike Samara with the Power Animal, the workbook didn't tell me anything about the Guardian Animal Spirit other than its name. This did not bother me much. I accepted that the shamanistic universe contains a number of features and entities whose nature and function do not vary significantly in their essence from one shamanistic voyager to the next, although their manifestations may differ widely and wildly. Presumably, the Guardian Animal Spirit was one of these, and its name would suffice to evoke it.

The workbook gave unusually lengthy, detailed instructions for this Journey. Unable to fit them easily into the three-part protocol that Samara had taught me, and unsure which part may be important to fix upon, I read the whole paragraph aloud as an announcement of my intention, all 141 words of it, all the while suspecting that this may not be the most effective mission statement.[9]

Despite fleeting images of what might have been treetops—wavy dark lines against a less dark background—none lasts long enough for me to feel sure I ever was in the Garden. I don't see the mound/burrow before I am in blackness. Nearly the whole Journey, I have no idea where I am. Am I on the way to the Lower World? Am I in the Lower World? Am I caught in the veil?

After a while, I do have a clear vision of passing through a round tunnel, rather rapidly, to judge by the rate at which its knobby, bumpy walls speed by. I descend through a number of twists and turns.

Here's a very large, very impressive, totemic, blackish bird. A raven? An owl? I ask who it is, but it does not answer. A variety of animal eyes appear out of the darkness and almost at once fade back into it, and also some human ones. There's a black silhouette of a cat's head against a whitish background, ears pointing up, then the cat's masked face, and its eyes gleam bright blue. It doesn't answer when I ask who it is. I think it may be Angel. I ask both the cat and the bird if either one is my Guardian, but neither responds, so I guess not. It would have been cool if it were Angel, I think.

---

9 In retrospect, "I want to go to the Lower World and find my Guardian Animal Spirit" probably would have done the trick, while bearing in mind the workbook's detailed description of what might occur and advice as to how to go about it. But as so often, I was struggling to find the right balance between controlling the Journey and surrendering to it; and my lawyerly tendency to niggle over verbiage and rules asserted itself.

Suddenly, a lot of imagery flashes before me, mostly contained in rectangular frames of light, like a movie montage running too fast to understand, some of it moving and some still, some of it involving dramatic explosions and orange flame.

I repeatedly call for my Guardian Animal Spirit to come to me. Nothing answers.

Maybe half a dozen times I see a light "ahead" of me, and I attempt to follow it or to go through it. For example, there's a rectangular opening that may be a door, but it also makes me think of the hearth in the House in the Garden. I move towards it, and I think I go through it, but it gets me nowhere.

At last, however, I see a blob of bluish, shifting, underwatery light that persists and expands to fill my whole field of vision as I approach and enter it. I wait there, floating in the light, calling for my Guardian Animal Spirit to join me, but I remain alone, so far as I can tell.

The drum hesitates, shifts into its "Journey's over" rhythm.

I retreat back into the blackness, thinking to return to my body the way I came, but now the blackness is different. During the Journey, before I found the underwatery light place, the blackness was like a screen on which visions played out (except for the passage through the tunnel—that had a 3D quality). Now I feel I am in the center of a spherical, crystalline space. The blackness has a quality of clarity and depth. I see faint, white glimmers where the space has its boundaries, hard-edged, linear, like the edges of a crystal's facets. It is kind of like being inside a quartz or diamond, if they were made of emptiness. It is nice in here, restful. That's where I am when the Journey ends.

27.

As Samara said, there is no such thing as a failed Journey. Every one teaches you something, or gives you something to meditate upon. Only much later would I come to recognize that, like previous Journeys, December 8 had introduced me to a number of Spirits and dreamworld features which I would meet again and learn more about on subsequent Journeys.

I continued struggling to understand just what were these Spirits I was encountering, the task given urgency by my need to know just what I was dealing with in the form of my grandmother. Following a trail that began in the anthology where I'd learned about the Malaysian shamans, I hunted down an obscure book by the British anthropologist Alan Tormaid Campbell, discussing his years of field work with the Wayãpí, a small, little-known Amazonian tribe.[10] Campbell's book reflects an admirable self-awareness regarding the practice of anthropology, the difficulties of ethnography, and the false, colonial/imperialist stance of superiority that pervades them, but it was a bit frustrating for me, since its concern with these issues often seems to eclipse the shamanic ideas that are so tantalizingly mentioned in its subtitle. But I found several nuggets. Campbell observes that the most fundamental difference between "us" and members of the Wayãpí tribe is that they live in a consciousness of connectedness to the world that is rooted in shamanism and that lacks the distinction "animate/inanimate" that is so basic to our quotidian worldview. He hypothesizes that "spirits are simply personified causes."

---

10 Alan Tormaid Campbell, *To Square with Genesis: Causal Statement and Shamanic Ideas in Wayãpí* (University of Iowa Press 1989)

Based on my admittedly limited experience thus far, I was inclined to substitute "relationships" for "causes" in Campbell's formulation. I thought, suppose what I perceive when shamanizing, the Spirits and other entities I interact with, are reified relationships?

Thinking about these attempts to pin down the nature of Spirits, and also about the teaching that the Middle World is coextensive with everything in the world of ordinary consciousness, this poem came to me,[11] as if to say, "Well, maybe, and look at it that way if you find it useful to do so, but there's more to it than that":

Reify This

"Yesterday, upon the stair,
I met a man who wasn't there
He wasn't there again today
I wish, I wish he'd go away . . ."

This ditty's up there in the attic
with "I wish I was an Oscar Mayer wiener"
and "I'm the jolly little baker
and you'll find me on the label
of Kaufman's rye bread"
and "I always do what's right
I never do anything wrong

11 It began when the opening quatrain, from Hughes Mearns' poem "Antigonish," inserted itself insistently in my consciousness. The rest followed in order: commercial ditties from a sausage manufacturer and a Western New York bakery; a song heard frequently on a children's television show of the 1950s; the title of the first book of poems I loved; the motto Don Marquis gave the cat Mehitabel in the second book of poems I loved; lines from e.e. cummings and Bob Dylan; and so on.

I'm a Romper Room do-bee
a do-bee all day long"

among a lot of boxes
stowed willy-nilly
some dusty-lidded some not
An old blanket chest
squeaks open and out pops
"There once was a puffin"
and "toujours gai toujours gai"
and "I sing of Olaf glad and big"

and in a battered cardboard crate nearby
"How many roads must a man walk down"
We sang to Sheila's strummed chords
in the back of the bus
within earshot of an old man
who enquired in reasonable tones
as if from a spirit of reasonable enquiry
which didn't hide anything
why don't you make your own songs

to which we had no answer
nor did we try to answer
it was one of those familiar questions
we were content to let hide
behind the curtain of Sheila's strumming
I wanted to kiss her
but never tried

28. December 15, 2021

At first, treetops. Then nothing but darkness and ambiguity, the sense of wandering aimlessly through caverns where I can see next to nothing. Fear, fear that I have lost it, that I'm blocked, that I'll never find my way in again.

Sparse, short, light brown hair, seen so close up the hairs look like limbless, fat, pointy saplings, the skin sandy-tan between them.

Someone lying in a bundle of brown robes; the robes are flung open, and I am invited to lie down with the person inside them. The gesture and invitation carry a feeling of protective affection, offering rest to the weary.

Something like an x-ray view of a person's rib cage and spine, in a dim, reddish light, a bright, crimson streak of a blood vessel running vertically through the otherwise empty cavity.

When the drum signals the Journey's end, I retreat, winding up in a clear, dark space much like the one where my last Journey ended. I realize it is a space under the trees in my Garden. After the drum falls silent, I resist the urge to flee back to normal consciousness, and I stay here a while, resting peacefully. Vague forms shift before my eyes with the colors and simple outlines of a Chagall in his more abstract mode. I like it here.

I come back to my body, feeling more refreshed and less spaced-out than usual, after a Journey.

Samara had said, two weeks ago, that a fragmented, incoherent Journey often is a sign that the mind is getting in its own way, trying too hard to dictate the experience or meet expectations. She had suggested a technique for dealing with this: if you feel you're going nowhere, visualize something as a way of jump-starting the Journey. So, this time, I had set out with a greatly simplified intention: go through my Garden to the Lower World and find my Guardian Spirit. During the Journey, I kept on telling myself to just let it happen.

Afterwards, I realized that I had been bearing down and giving directions every inch of the way. I hadn't seen the Garden's treetops right off, so I made myself see them. I didn't see the grassy mound that I thought contained the entrance to the Lower World, so I tried to visualize it, and when that didn't work, I tried to visualize the tunnel that I thought I should be in, and when that didn't work, I began calling out for my Guardian Spirit to come to me. All the while telling myself I was relaxing into the flow! I was sure this was not what Samara had meant by "jump-starting the Journey."

This is tricky stuff. I was all too prone to try to force my way in to the shamanic world. Paradoxically, I also was afraid of committing to it once it unfolds. Yes, it is about control, and fear of losing same, but there's more.

I thought of the decades I had spent learning to listen for a poem, learning to recognize it when it comes and not to confuse it with a mere idea formed of words, learning to take the time to dress a poem in the language that best fits it, and to hold the poem gently but firmly so as neither to kill it nor to let it escape before it is done. Perhaps shamanizing requires a similar skill set.

Perhaps, I thought, I had been trying too hard on this Journey due to writing-related pressures. Did the fear of being blocked out of the dreamworld reflect my association of shamanizing with this writing project, that had rescued me from a lengthy, maybe endless fallow period? What pain, what a sense of defeat, what loss of my place in the world, if this were to come to nothing!

But it never comes to nothing. Some substance had leaked through my mental interference. This Journey had posed questions for which I could have no answers without Journeying again. Who was that, hidden in the robes? Who have I seen who was dressed like that? Was it my grandmother? Is she my Guardian Spirit? Should I have accepted her invitation to lie down with her, instead of shying away? Was she also the subject of the x-ray? Was that an invitation to know her from the inside? If so, what could that possibly mean?

29. December 17, 2021

On the basis of something I read on a web site, I decided that I needed to Journey much more frequently if I wanted to develop a firm connection to wherever it was that I was going. Because when had the internet ever steered me wrong? My willingness to resort to it was an index of my deep discouragement. I barely considered the possibility that, in fact, the Spirits were taking me where they wanted me to go, proceeding at their own deliberate pace, and that I was like a swimmer who furiously waves his arms and waggles his legs, convinced he is drowning, while the lifeguard patiently tows him to shore.

I decided also to cut back drastically my pre-Journey ritual. It definitely did help to establish a mental space for shamanizing, but maybe it also was a symptom of trying too hard. As I now contemplated Journeying as frequently as daily or at least weekly, the very thought of performing the full ritual each time felt so cumbersome as to threaten the sustainability of the enterprise. So, for the time being, anyway, I'd dispense with the Six Directions and the shofar blasts and the careful enunciation of my intended itinerary, and see how that worked. I'd still smudge the room, though. Sage smudge smells so nice.

On the subject of nice odors, something strange had happened this morning, while I was meditating. I'd meditated regularly for the past twenty years. Retirement made it easier to maintain a routine. I'd listen to the BBC World Service, then, when it was over, light some incense and sit. Usually, the smoke rose straight up from the stick. Even when the heat came on, creating air currents in my otherwise still living room, that vertical grey line would be disrupted only mildly and momentarily. Today, however, for the duration of the session, the smoke had flowed horizontally, directly at me, floating lazily in swirls and curlicues and small, ghostly sheets, as if it were bowing to me, or as if someone were blowing sweetness at me. It was lovely. It was dizzying.

In the afternoon, I walked to the grocery to buy some milk and cream cheese. On the way there, despite my resolution not to wordsmith a mission statement, my mind went over and over it, carefully composing. I wanted to go to the Lower World. Despite my better judgment, despite Samara's advice, I couldn't be content with just saying that. Multiple formulae revolved through me. I got hung up on whether I should specify that I would go "through my Garden," or maybe I should say, "go to my Garden, find the portal to the Lower World, and go there," or should I add, "and look around," or maybe, "and find my Guardian Spirit," or, "talk with the robed woman." Thirty years a lawyer, and this is what you get.

Something much more significant happened during that walk, in one of the few intervals when I wasn't obsessing over the phrases spinning before me on my language turntable.

In a moment of leakage between this world and the Spirit World, I had a brief mental exchange with the robed woman who was my grandmother. You know, the kind of internal dialogue in which your interlocutor, who appears out of nowhere, comes up with her lines on her own. I asked her, "What do you want?" The response: "I want you to let me love you."

On the way home, walking up Dorset Street towards Williston Road, a tree caught my attention. I wasn't sure what species. Not very tall, it had gnarly branches and dark bark, but of course at this time of year it was bare of leaves. Maybe it was dead. I didn't think so, not altogether, even though it had been grievously injured, split down the middle to ground level. Perhaps it had been struck by lightning, or weakened by disease, or a strong wind had found a structural flaw. About five feet up, near the top of the split, a metal rod held the halves together. You wouldn't do that for a dead tree, you'd cut it down. On a lot of the branches the bark had a smoothness, a lighter color, that indicated recent growth. The main trunk, branched out just above eye level, just above the metal rod, was a cylinder split lengthwise, the halves leaning apart, the former heartwood rotted away, the remaining sapwood weathered brown and curved like half-pipes. The trunk's bark covered it tightly, not peeling away or dropped off as it would if there were no life beneath it. At the very bottom, the trunk's halves joined, forming a cup which embraced a soft-looking bed of wood chips and flakes. I stared into it. Until now, I had not felt strongly that I had found a good portal into the Lower World. This tree, at once both living and dead, could draw me down.

But I had encountered the tree in ordinary reality, not in my Garden. I thought, Wendy's workbook said to find the Lower World through the Garden. Then I thought, everything in my world is in the Garden. I did not think to ask myself why, if Badger had shown me already the way through his burrow, I needed any other portal.

In the event, I laid me down, put in my earbuds, clicked on the drumming, and muttered, almost as an afterthought, "Going to the Lower World." I visualized the tree.

I undergo a bout of nervous are-we-there-yets, like a kid in the back seat way too early in the road trip. I picture the tree several times, impatiently bouncing back to it from the amorphous darkness I sink into each time. I try to follow blobs and patches of light. Catching myself doing this, I remind myself to be still and let it come to me.

I'm in a swamp. Lots of water, dense thicket, stunted, stick-like trees. Not the dead of night, but sometime near sunset. Passing out of the swamp through woods that remind me of the Garden. Misty, small lakes with jagged shorelines and small, tree-plumed islands, like the Canadian boreal forest. I look across rows of ridges under a sunset, dusky-pink sky. Reminded again of the Garden, I wonder if there is grassland here, but I don't see any.

A big red face, like a cartoon Satan, occupies most of my field of vision, but its features are obscured by a veil of some sort. I tell it to "show" itself, meaning to reveal its identity, but it doesn't. It goes away.

A tiny, pale orb hangs in the sky for a moment, a star or planet as if seen through a haze. It disappears and I feel chills. They don't go away. I am feeling fearful. I call on Mama Bear to lend me strength. She does, and having done so, departs. I watch her eyes and snout dwindle into the distance. I feel calm and confident again. I thank Mama Bear.

Although I'd told myself I wouldn't do so on this trip, I call for my Guardian Spirit a couple of times. No answer. I resume letting it happen around me.

There's a long-furred, English sheepdog, all white and grey fringes. It playfully leaps around me, turning its head towards me. "Who are you? What's your name?" I ask.

"Phoebe," she answers.

"Are you my Guardian Spirit?"

"Yes."

"Who is the robed woman?"

"Your maternal grandmother."

I ask Phoebe to take me to this Spirit, but she's already leaving. I try to follow her, but I can't. I want to thank her, to ask what service I can do her, what I might offer her out of gratitude for her assistance (all as prescribed in the workbook for such a moment), but she's gone.

I think, if Phoebe is my Guardian Spirit, then that confirms that the robed woman isn't: she hadn't said she was.

30. December 20, 2021

I had planned to start the Journey about 3:30 p.m., a little before sunset at this time of year, where I live. I spent the earlier part of the afternoon composing a letter to the corporate capitalistic beast that squats atop a hill near my house, masquerading as a hospital. By the time 3:30 rolled around, I was still steaming. After pacing around the house, torn as to whether it was a good idea to go ahead in that frame of mind, I impulsively smudged my Journeying room. I smudged it very thickly. The sweet scent got me smiling. I blew a few blasts on the shofar, just to make noise, then flopped down on the bed, put in my earbuds, and triggered the music.

The first sign that something is amiss is my inability to visualize the portal tree, despite trying over and over. I realize I have not stated any intention. I mutter, "Go to Lower World."

A lot of nothingness ensues. an indeterminate, in-between space. Animals are there: an owl, a wolf, monkeys, perhaps a hawk. Briefly, there's a tunnel, into which I both go and do not go.

Then I see treetops silhouetted against the sky, and I know I am in the Lower World. I start calling to Phoebe, as if she were an actual dog, "Here, Phoebe. Here, Phoebe." She fails to show up.

Instead of Phoebe, I see a little man's face in profile. He is like an elf. We don't speak. I see a little, round house in the distance, a brown, cylindrical structure with no windows and a thatch roof. I see a woman lying on her side with her back to me, a pose like that of Scarlett Johansen at the beginning of the movie "Lost in Translation," but her bottom and thighs are bare. Her thighs shift slightly. But she is not the most vivid image of this disconnected series. That is the one it ends with. It is a very big house with a high, peaked roof, like a very large A-frame ski cottage. A row of windows across the front glows. It is a dark night. I am downslope from the house, looking up. I look at it for a while, watching for movement, but I see none. Again I call for Phoebe as if she were an actual dog. "Here, Phoebe. Here, Phoebe."

31.

Thinking of what to say about the December 20 Journey, it was obvious to me that I had been disrespectful towards Phoebe, treating her as a regular dog and not as a Spirit Guide, and that this was not the way to approach the dreamworld and its Spirits. Perhaps I drew the conclusion, unconsciously and figuratively, that if one does not, if one disses them, one winds up with egg on one's face. Anyway, this poem came to me:

Humpty Dumpty

From his perch atop a mortarless
wall, the fragments of a long-dead
noble's castle artlessly piled
to keep the cabbages safe from cows,

Humpty Dumpty sings the morning
up above a distant line of
trees that fringe the distant horizon
like eyelashes. He betters the cock by

singing sounds of his own devising,
not a stale, genetically encoded
EWR-er-ER-er-ERRRRR, and not
consensual reality's

formulaic paeans; rather,
filling words with secret intentions,
he flings them like water balloons,
happily careless of embarrassing

nearby bystanders who can't quite catch
the meanings; hums a tune as random
as sunspots. In his uncaged joy,
he reaches back to uncork a big one,

reaches back a bit too far;
unbalanced, topples. What he'd had
within him now spreads slowly, glistens
at long last for all to see.

32. Last week of December, 2021

I tried to return to the Lower World to make things right with Phoebe by approaching her with more respect. Although I thought I probably had gotten to the right place, since there was at one point a brief vision of sliding down a twisting tunnel and much later I saw the swamp, a midnight blue, watery waste, prickly with limbless, stunted tree-stalks, there was no Phoebe and not much of anything else.

I had a hunch that having met my Guardian Animal, even though I had accomplished less than what Wendy's workbook recommended for this encounter, most notably a dialogue about what we could do for each other, maybe I should just move on to the next workbook exercise as if the last one had been completed successfully. I invited Phoebe to join me in my Garden for "conversation."

Instead of finding Phoebe, I wander inside a building stuffed with bric-a-brac and old furniture, like one of those "antique shops" one finds throughout rural New England, full of oil lamps with frilly, frosted glass chimneys, two-drawer desks, bed frames leaning randomly against overstuffed chairs, and other aged household objects slightly too good for yard sales. (Is it the House where I lit the hearth? Is it the A-frame? Some other dwelling? Whose? I don't think to ask, "Why do the Spirits keep taking me to such places?")

Oddly, while browsing this dusty, musty merchandise, every once in a while, I am startled by a flashing vision of treetops. I wonder how I could be seeing them from inside the building. I pose this as a question to the building. Its answer, "They're outside," isn't particularly helpful. I recall that I might be in both places at once, but that doesn't seem helpful, either. I ask, "Is Phoebe here?

"Yes," the building replies.

"Where?" I ask.

"Upstairs."

Okay, I try to go upstairs. I see no staircase and can't produce a feeling of ascent, but somehow I get to a set of rooms that somehow I know are upstairs. I search through them. No Phoebe.

Mainly, other than that, it is a light show of formshifting blobs.

My discouragement deepened. It seemed as if the door, once narrowly ajar just enough for me to sneak through and since then slowly creaking open, had shut.

33.

Shocked by the robed woman I had seen on December 15, her pleas for love, her hug, her invitation to share her garment, I had retreated into the workbook. I realized that, although it had served admirably until now as a curriculum, instead, at this juncture it had become a trap. Focused on the workbook, I had been avoiding the lessons the Spirits had for me. Those lessons centered on her. The choice was simple. I could do the work the Spirits had set out for me, or I could flounder in bewilderment until I gave up. That's the way I thought about it. In moments when this struck me as perhaps ascribing too much agency to "the Spirits, whatever they actually are," I thought of it another way, more congenial to my background as a lawyer and investigator. In sticking to the workbook, I was pursuing a line of enquiry that was proving unproductive, failing to follow the evidence. Same difference.

Likewise, in this chronicle of my education, there is no way forward except through her. When I first had met the robed woman, I decided to refer directly to the defining complication of that part of my history which she represented only if I could not tell this story without doing so, and then only in the vaguest possible terms. At that time, I had not anticipated the extent to which my project would compel me to engage in any such discussion. But let me make it clear: in doing so now, I am sticking as closely as I can to my original decision. This is not an autobiography. This chronicle's only subject is my education in shamanism.

That said . . . it is time to tell you about two climactic moments. The first occurred in the early 1980s. I had been prompted to go into psychotherapy by a horrible weekend when I suddenly for no apparent reason became terrified of every human interaction. Nothing like this ever had happened to me, nor has it since. After a couple of days of being unable to go to the corner store and buy a can of soup without mustering all the courage and self-control I possessed, I forced myself to telephone the Employee Assistance Program at the university where I was working. They referred me to Robert Rossel, Ph.D.

If you have worked with a gifted therapist, you will have some idea what I owe to this insightful, perceptive, intelligent, sweet man. It came to a head (so to speak) after a year or so, when he leaned back in his chair, looked at me gravely, and said, "I am sorry to have to be the one to tell you this, Seth, but there is nothing wrong with you." They say comedy is all about timing. His was perfect. It released a torrent of gasping, wrenching sobs from me, a flood of grief and relief that washed away an immeasurably immense weight I had been carrying.

A few years after my first course of work with Rob, I returned to him for help in learning to deal with the heavy stresses of new parenthood. There came a time when he drew my attention to a characteristic gesture of mine. My back would arch slightly, and I would hold my arms out to each side, elbows bent at right angles, hands raised straight up, palms forward. What did this mean, he asked? Apart from associating the gesture with feelings of surprise, helplessness, and dismissal, I did not have an immediate answer. He helped me look for one. He did not suggest in even the subtlest of ways what that answer might be. It was hidden. His job was to help me find it. When I did, after weeks of searching, it broke forth with an astonishing force of pain. If that first moment of reassurance that I wasn't defective had elicited a flash flood, this was a dam bursting. After the waters receded, we spent many months clearing the rubble.

The memory was more somatic than cerebral. I felt it to be connected with my maternal grandmother and my preschool years. She had been helping my parents care for me. Something had occurred, traumatic in nature, vast in importance. What exactly this event consisted of, I could not say with any confidence, other than that I associated it with my grandmother. The memory of it had been buried entirely, until that day when Rob helped me unearth what remained.

It was the late 1980s. Awareness of sexual abuse of children had recently dawned upon American society, rapidly becoming pervasive (as was and is the problem itself). I became convinced that I had resurfaced the remnants of a memory of my grandmother handling me inappropriately.

From then on, Rob's therapy proceeded consistently with the newly evolved and prevailing standards of sensitivity to the needs of child sexual abuse victims to be heard and accepted, to be freed of the crushing bonds of denial. He recommended a book by Mike Lew, *Victims No Longer,* published just a year or two before, in which I saw much of myself, and which was quite helpful. Eventually, we got me around to disclosing to my mother the recollection of having been violated by her mother. My mother reacted instantly. She said, "I'm so sorry," and embraced me. I could not have asked for better.

In short, I had received therapeutic treatment of great skillfulness, sophistication, and sensitivity, and when I had burst out of denial and disclosed my troubling past, I had been greeted with unhesitating acceptance and love. I believed my recovery to be complete. Then why, so many years later, had the robed woman come to me in trance? Why, despite my sentimental moment of forgiveness, did she continue to trouble me with her demands to "let me love you" and her ambiguous, borderline creepy "physical" overtures? What was unresolved?

Doubts began to stir. In the back of my mind, in the dark places, rested suspicions that my mother's support had been too unconditional, too quick, too easy. Was it a cover-up for some guilt of her own? Did she have some role in this? These were queasy thoughts. Was there something other than molestation that had motivated me, as a toddler, to develop a lifelong revulsion for the woman who had tried to help my mother care for me? I was bedrock certain only that something had happened, and that it involved my grandmother.

I contemplated that robed woman's pleas. Do you love me? Will you accept the intimacy of my robes? Will you let me love you? The first had been not only her question, but mine as well. Even if there were more to the story than I had believed, even if her role in it should turn out to lack moral culpability, how could I love a person from whom all my life I had felt so profoundly estranged? How could I trust her Spirit? My immediate reaction to her invitation to be enwrapped in her robes had been suspicion. I had pulled away from her mentally, rather the way a horse will shy at a snake in its path, even though I had felt no menace coming from her, nothing but affection and protectiveness. I was afraid of being "physically" close and vulnerable to her. I had recoiled from the UR-violation, whatever it was, that had defined and marred our history. Could I let her Spirit love me (whatever that may mean) even if I wanted to, or was that possibility foreclosed by such reflexive revulsion no matter what its genesis?

I thought about the person with whom I was dealing. It sounds meaningful to say that Spirits are reified relationships, but that merely locates the phenomenon, omitting an essential aspect of the matter, which is that Spirits manifest as persons. This particular person's love for her eldest grandchild had been thwarted at least since 1975, when she had died, and probably for approximately 20 years of life before that, a blockage that now underlaid the most urgent message of her being.

I remembered the year and a half that had led up to my divorce, the unremitting, bone-deep ache of loving someone who has stopped accepting it. With much labor, my former spouse and I had salvaged a friendship from the wreckage. With perseverance and mutual goodwill, through our friendship once again had begun a modest flow of love of a non-marital variety, deepening over the years, that I now counted as one of the great blessings of my life.

Leaping to the assumption that Spirits are capable of feeling pain, I tried to imagine the robed woman's. I began to feel that I could accept her love, and the pain that accompanied it, if she could accept the same from me. If I was going to let her love me, that love would have to include all the pain I associated with her, and all its ramifications in my life. That was the deal she would have to make.

So, it was compassion that did it. One day, I was beginning my morning meditation. I sat down on the bench, folded my legs, rested my hands palm up on my thighs in the "gyan mudra" posture. My breath came and went, evenly, a bit shallow. I followed it in and out, eyes closed, feeling my back straighten and my head rise into a relaxed but erect position. I opened my eyes, inhaling a thick whiff of incense. The smoke was drifting diagonally across the room, to my right, spreading out to send me the occasional waft. I felt moved to do something quite unusual. I slowly raised my arms and held them out before me, slightly rounded as if in a hug. From my coccyx on the bench to the top of my head, I felt unusually alive. Maintaining the hug, I murmured, yes, I will let you love me. It mildly surprised me to hear me say it and to feel that I meant it. The smoke shifted, directly at me.

Now for the poem. For several years, a few dear friends and I had been gathering weekly to play board games. It had helped us to preserve our sanity through the lockdowns and social distancing of the pandemic. During the past year, I had described for them my Journeys each week they occurred. It was a way out of another sort of isolation. With this poem, I was ready to answer a question one of them had asked long ago:

"Why did you have to leave your childhood
through a window," my friend Wendy Sue,
perceptive as the poet she is

not, persistently inquisitive
as the scientist she is, wants to
know each time I fall silent after

having told the four of them gathered
around the old, oak table a new
instalment in the ongoing saga

of my cranial adventures, and
each time I reserve my answer for
the day when I might have one, until

this day, illuminated by love,
I know I had to use the window
because more customary exits

had been blocked to me long before I
ever might have found them, and I could
not bear to stay within forever.

34. January 13, 2022

I called on Mama Bear and her cubs, invoking their spirit of playful strength, and my Guardian Spirit, Phoebe, to support and protect me in my visit to the Middle World for the purpose of communicating with the robed woman.

Right away, I'm in the woods, standing in the middle of a small, circular clearing surrounded by tall pines, in that familiar dusk. I have the sense that I am in a sacred space. I stay there awhile, until it dissolves to a path through the trees. I walk a long time. Although it remains dark beneath the foliage, which here is deciduous, a bright blue, daylight sky shines above the leaves.

I enter among a number of buildings, dark, seemingly uninhabited structures of unpainted, rough planks and logs: cabins, stables, a crude house with a porch. I wander in and out of some of them, not seeing much.

Then I enter a house that is different. It is rather nice, an old-fashioned, middle-class dwelling. At the top of the foyer's wall opposite the entrance, there's a decorative, semicircular mirror.

"Are you here?" I ask.

"Yes."

"Where?"

"In the basement."

I go to the basement. This doesn't involve going down stairs. It involves being in a black space and concentrating on going to the basement. "Where are you?"

"In the corner."

"Which corner? Show me." It's very dark in the basement.

"Here," she says. I see a rectangular opening, a

bulkhead door to the outside. "Come to me through it," she indicates.

I exit the basement into a beautiful flower garden. I don't actually see the flowers, just the outlines of shrubs, but I know that's what it is. The sky is a lovely, dusty pink. I walk in the garden. It is rather larger than the average suburban backyard. In front of me flashes a brilliant, red, climbing rose. A brilliant, red chrysanthemum explodes before me, like a firework.

A series of bright, sharp images pass before me, forming and dissolving too rapidly for recognition. I have the feeling of being told more than I can absorb. Suddenly, I see with extreme clarity a brightly lit, tan, concrete, basement sink with a gleaming, chrome faucet. I have the sense that it is used for washing clothing, or diapers. I see a similarly sharply focused, brightly lit segment of a wall, a basement wall of concrete blocks. I realize that she has been showing me places that she has lived. She is showing me bits of her life.

The drum changes its rhythm. "Goodbye, Grandma," I say.

After I had jotted down my notes of this Journey, I felt good. I smiled. This had been a success. I had guessed correctly what I needed to do. By doing it, I had broken through to the "getting to know you" stage of the relationship. She had given me a bouquet, and had been showing me images of her life as people becoming friends share anecdotes. I wondered if she was privy to details of my life, just by virtue of what she was, whereas I would have to obtain knowledge of her little by little, because of what I am.

I got up to make a cup of tea. In the kitchen, I leaned against the counter, and happy tears filled my eyes.

35.

On a bitterly frigid Friday afternoon in January, I drove the 36 miles from my home in South Burlington to Montpelier, Vermont, for a long-awaited meeting with Wendy Halley. Cold and covid had emptied State Street, so it was easy to park right across from Wendy's office.

Entering, I found a woman working at a computer in a corner of the small, pleasantly colorful, casually furnished room. It could have been a corner coffee shop, with a comfy couch and chairs, a bookshelf on one wall, a couple of beautifully painted hoop drums on the other wall. She welcomed me in and continued with whatever it was she was doing. We kept our masks on. I took some time removing my coat, sweater, gloves, and scarf, and hanging them on a hook in the hall. Then she led me to a room in the back of the suite, mildly cluttered (but uncrowded) with books and furniture and miscellaneous objects, its lighting subdued. Bookishness: a reader. The space's informality was relaxing to me. Sitting opposite each other in well-worn, upholstered easy chairs, we began.

She asked me what I was looking for from this meeting. I said that I had a million questions. I could continue to stumble along more or less on my own, but I thought I could learn my way through the dreamworld more efficiently with an experienced teacher. I described how I had helped Samara with her homework assignment; how this had intrigued me to want to learn to do what Samara was doing; how I'd visited the House in my Garden, talked with the House, lit the hearth; how my grandmother had intercepted me on the way to the Lower World; how we had begun to reconcile.

I liked the way that Wendy listened. Her questions were

few and to the point. She asked if I thought my work with my grandmother was finished. I said that whatever had been standing between us seemed to be resolved, but I didn't know what she might become to me going forward. I've been agonizing over what to do on my next Journey, I said. Go back to the workbook? Revisit Grandma, maybe ask her what in fact had happened to alienate us? I liked the way that Wendy did not answer directly. Instead, she nodded, as if to say yes, those are things you could do. Which turned out to be what I had wanted to know.

Wendy told me about her background as a Master's degree psychologist and psychotherapist, the spontaneous visionary experiences that had led her to the Hawaiian shamanic tradition as taught by Hank Wesselman. I told her what a great relief it was, to be able to speak with someone who knew what the hell I was talking about. I said, it must have been incredibly difficult for her, carrying a shamanic consciousness into a culture so overwhelmingly ignorant of it, so hostile to its perspective and uses.

Wendy asked me again what I wanted from this session. I said that although I had a million questions, I didn't know how to organize them. She offered to give me the overall framework that her teachers had given her, beyond the bare outlines sketched in her workbook. Yes, that would be helpful, I said. If she had asked, I could not have told her in what way it would be helpful. I bathed in her offer of a common language, a common perspective, a means of comprehending what was important for me to know.

Before getting into it any further, though, I need to add a caveat: what follows is not in any way intended as an authoritative account of Hawaiian shamanism. (Indeed, nothing in this book is so intended.) Transmission from one culture of its central philosophies, traditions, practices, and beliefs, to another culture in which those mental constructs have no living counterpart, is a tricky business at best. The generation of anthropologists that included Michael Harner and Hank Wesselman had begun to put into practice their suspicion that these shamans they had been studying might be onto something worth investigating on its own merits and in its own terms. They had placed their shamanistic explorations within the context of their anthropological scholarship, having no other framework. But deriving a worldview from someone else's tradition is not the same as partaking of that tradition. To preserve its own integrity, a culture imposes a myriad of self-corrective mechanisms on those operating within it. These do not apply to persons borrowing its ideas and practices from outside. There's an immense amount of room for misinterpretation, creative transformation, and adaptation relatively unhindered by group norms and consensual ideation.

One might say that, if Wesselman was a first-generation immigrant from the West to the Polynesian shamanistic milieu, his student Wendy Halley is of the second generation. Wendy does not pretend to be an expert in Hawaiian spirituality and philosophy. (Her honesty about this is one of the things I value about her. For example, she insisted on this caveat.) She has received a mental framework grounded in these knowledge systems, as transmitted to her by Hank Wesselman, which is useful to her for understanding her personal experience; for pursuing her own, shamanistic practice; and for teaching others about shamanism.

Place me, then, in the third generation. Coincidentally, I am in the third generation of Jewish immigrants to America. I might learn some Yiddish, but I never will know what it was like to live in a Ukrainian shtetl, and my Judaism is of a flavor that probably would be close to unrecognizable to those who did live there, although derived from what they brought here with them. My point is that even someone in the direct line of transmission may be far from the original teachings. Which is to say, I accept total responsibility for any errors or distortions in representing what Wendy passed on to me.

Reality, said Wendy, exists on a number of levels. For convenience, we talk about them as if they were separate and discrete from one another, but the truth of the matter is that they all occur together and at once. "Level is a matter of focus," she said. The Hawaiians posit four main levels.

The first level is physical or "objective" reality. This is the world as we experience it in our daily lives. Everything in this reality is separate from everything else. Everything has a beginning and an ending. Causes have effects.

The second level is subjective or "psychic" reality. Here we are talking about thoughts, emotions, feelings, energy. On this level, everything is connected by, exists within, and forms part of a matrix. Hawaiians call this matrix "aka". There is no such thing as time on the second level. There are no beginnings and endings, only cycles and transitions.

The third level is the one with which shamanism is most concerned. This "dreamtime," as Wendy preferred to call it, is all about symbolism. Everything in the dreamtime is symbolic. Wendy said that shamanism is an education in the interpretation of symbols.

I replied that, as a poet, I don't find it difficult to interpret symbols; it's generating them that can give me problems. I said I had gotten the idea from reading people's accounts of their shamanic Journeys that it would be like watching a movie, a continuous, narrative flow of moving images. Instead, in my experience, images flashed and disappeared, and I had to infer the meanings and connections that they indicated more or less clearly, mixed with short stretches of more cinematic continuity and then stretches of incoherent, amorphous, shifting blobs of color.

Wendy did not say, it should be like this or that. She thought for a moment, then said that the colors often are a result of being anxious, or trying too hard, or letting one's analytic mind or expectations interfere. (Guilty on all counts!)

Everything in the dreamtime, said Wendy, is part of a pattern and exists in relationship: "everything means what you think it means." She was not suggesting that the third level of reality is purely subjective; far from it. Her axiom carries a meaning more complicated than it sounds. I thought of William Blake's proverb, "Everything possible to be believed is an image of truth."

The third level consists in turn of three differing manifestations, or three Worlds. The three Worlds, like the four levels, represent interpenetrating, co-occurring phenomena.[12]

The Middle World is congruent with daily experience, the contents of quotidian consciousness. It is "the dreaming of the physical universe." It contains everything that inhabits our lives, and that we inhabit. From reality as we ordinarily experience it, to the Middle World, is a lateral move.

The Lower World is "the dreaming of nature." Here are the Spirits of all things that have ever lived, mythological creatures and other archetypes, and the elements. Wendy named the elements, adding one to the four we are used to: "earth, water, air, fire, and metal."

In the Upper World, which Wendy also called "home," resides one's Higher Self, the immortal part of one's being.

---

12 I found this idea instantly congenial. In the final verses of the last canto of *Once Was Lost*, concluding book of my trilogy *In Dante's Wake*, written some years before I met Wendy Halley, the narrator's focus literally shifts from level to level, World to World. While it does not exactly follow the Hawaiian schema, it is, I think, a remarkable example of the propinquity between poetic inspiration and shamanic perception.

Having said which, she immediately quashed one set of potential implications by adding, "There's nothing human about the Upper World." Journeying there, one might meet ancestors, ascended masters, great teachers. "But I met my grandmother on the border between the Middle World and the Lower World," I objected. "I'll get to that," said Wendy. But she didn't do so directly. The answer was implicit in what followed.

Wendy paused. What she was about to say, she told me, was her own observation, not something she had received from her teachers. "The Spirit World is pure consciousness," she said. As I write this, the words sound abstract, almost trite. But I remember their impact in the moment. I was not receiving a philosophical proposition. I was being shown a map. I can't ascribe any useful, discursive meaning to the phrase, "the Spirit World is pure consciousness;" on the other hand, it denotes a location that I recognize, having been there. Wendy continued: the Middle World represents "who you think you are at that time;" the Lower World represents both one's own and the collective unconscious, and is where healing happens; the Upper World is higher consciousness, one's "Higher Self," where the "big questions" such as "what is my purpose" and "what happens after death" may find answers. The Spirit World, on the whole, is INFORMATION. I write it this way because she said it this way each of the several times she said it during our session.

The dreamtime, or Spirit World, is "the real world," said Wendy. Events in the Spirit World manifest later as changes in our quotidian existence. She said that she had begun to suspect that ordinary consciousness, not the shamanic trance state, "is the dream world."

I turned this around and around in my mind. In light of my dawning acquaintance with the dreamworld, I could see why Wendy felt this way, but I wondered about it. After all, interactions do not, indeed cannot run in only one set of directions among the various levels of reality and among the Worlds. For that reason alone, it seemed questionable to ascribe priority to any of them. On the other hand, Wendy certainly had more experience with this stuff than I did! Perhaps, I thought, by turning "reality" on its head, Wendy was aiming at something other than a mere reversal of the hierarchical model which serves ordinary consciousness in its dominance of our perception of daily life. Another way of hearing her was to be reminded that whatever level of whatever World we are dealing with, the thing we are dealing with is our life.

A few days later, taking a break from writing up my notes of the session with Wendy, I came across this meditation by Corine Sombrun, a French master of shamanistic trance in the Mongolian tradition:

> Does there exist a cause-and-effect relation between the dreamtime and reality? At least, in that the dreamtime also may be a form of reality. Of two parallel realities. Or of a single vision from two different perspectives.[13]

Wendy described briefly a fourth World, the Holistic World. Here, there is no sense of self. All is one. It corresponds to the delta wave patterns observed in EEG readings of people in the deepest state of sleep.

---

13 My translation. "Existe-t-il une relation de cause à effet entre ce rêve et la réalité? À moins que ce rêve soit aussi une forme de la réalité. De deux réalités parallèles. Ou d'une seule vue de deux perspectives différentes." Corine Sombrun, *La Diagonale de la Joie: Voyage au cœur de la transe* (Editions Albin Michel 2021), p. 150

Before we parted, Wendy dismissed an anxiety probably common to beginners. The literature of shamanism is replete with descriptions of nastiness and danger that one might run into. For example, Corine Sombrun reports that a Mongolian shaman's costume is intended as a sort of elaborate armor against supernatural attackers, malevolent Spirits that may be acting on their own or as the agents of evil shamans, and that, so it is said, may psychically or even physically maim, kill, or possess their target, or block him or her from returning to ordinary consciousness. Wendy said that she had never encountered any such thing in her several decades of practice. So far as she was concerned, they do not exist. She believed that stories of such misadventures are the products of fear and superstition. It no longer struck me as ironic that a shamanic practitioner would draw the line at superstition. We talked about some of the entities I had crossed paths with, that you'd think would have been terrifying. I said they had not scared me at the times that I had met them. They had disappeared from view almost as soon as I had looked at them fixedly, or Mama Bear had swept them away on my behalf. There had been the fish in the icy stream snarling at me with their long, skewer-like teeth, the praying mantis/tyrannosaurus suddenly looming over me in the childhood House. "Cool," said Wendy, when I told her about the latter. I agreed.

Then Wendy gave me this final thought. Indicating the body parts with her hands, she said that it is not the head, but rather the heart and belly from which Journeying proceeds best, with "the pure, sweet innocence of childhood."

Back in 2004, I had written this poem. It came to mind now, seventeen years later, as I thought about this world and that World and which might really be real:

When I am Awake

When I am awake
my body rests, ready.
When I am awake
I know my dream.
When I am awake
a silent stream carries words.
When I am awake
I see the other people.
When I am awake
I watch and wonder.
When I am awake
I love and do not seek love.
When I am awake
I am grateful for you.
When I am awake
pain is one of my two oars.
When I am awake
call and I will row over.
When I am awake

36. January 27, 2022

Treetops, at first dark and fuzzy. A point of light glares through them, casting long, sharp rays. It is the sun, in a blue sky, piercing dense foliage. The treetops rush by overhead. I am looking continuously up at them. Why so fast? I am hurrying to meet her. I begin to see the green of the uppermost leaves, that were just black silhouettes at the outset. Gradually, the pace slows. I come to a stop in a small clearing. Is she there? I ask her what happened, way back when I was little. Behind that question is another: what can we be to each other now? I do not see her or hear her. I see lots of faces, they come and go one or two at a time. Among them, I glimpse Mama Bear! Mostly women, some men. There's a thin, white-faced man with a sharp chin and long, pointy mustachios that wave as if in a breeze. There are other people I also don't recognize. After a while I realize that she is communicating through images about the people she was among, long ago. There's my mother; I know her eyes are lowered, though her eyelids are shut. A somewhat stylized rendering, but it's her, young. There my mother is with her mother. My grandmother's arm is around my mom's shoulders, affectionately. There is a mouth distorted in a howl of pain and grief. There is a woman's breast, with an erect nipple. I see it again, or is it another? There is my mother from the waist up, lying on her back. Her body is a mosaic of little black and blue squares. There follow many images too fleeting or not quite within my frame of visual reference or vocabulary, although some of them, particularly the several honey-golden colored ones, are quite bright, sharp and detailed. Metallic surfaces, flat or curved? One of them is partly covered with tiny, decorative pyramids set in regular rows and columns, like on a grid. A piece of jewelry? A ring, or bracelet, or brooch? It is as if I am watching her thoughts and can't quite make them out. "You're talking too fast," I say, "I don't speak Yiddish." She is sorting through all her memories. A lot happened that had nothing to do with me. It comes to this, she says, or I say and she confirms: she doesn't know what estranged us, and she is finished with me, in the sense that there is nothing more to say. Sadness, acceptance.

37.

Although by this time I had stopped looking to biology for answers about the nature of what I was meeting in the dreamworld, neuroscience now resurfaced as an aid to interpreting what the Spirits were teaching me.

Corine Sombrun presents a theory of the neurobiology of trance grounded in childhood brain development.[14] She starts with the hypothesis that trance is an innate brain capacity which is inhibited by the operation of ordinary consciousness. To this, she adds the observation that a part of the brain necessary to ordinary consciousness, namely the prefrontal cortex, lacks development in an infant up to the age of two or three years. Cortical development proceeds in stages. It is not complete until the mid-twenties. Until the cortex matures beyond infancy and early childhood, so Sombrun's theory goes, the child's consciousness consists of what, in an adult, would be considered a trance. As the prefrontal cortex and other features of the brain mature, certain neural connections, including many of those involved in manifesting trance, are downgraded or eliminated in favor of preserving, maintaining, and extending networks now more heavily used and more immediately pertinent to survival. Ordinary consciousness takes over as the default medium for awareness. The capacity for trance does not disappear, however, and can be re-established and used by the adult brain when the inhibitions imposed by ordinary consciousness are lifted, for example, in extreme situations, or by the voluntary act of a shamanic practitioner.

Another major neurological event occurs at about the same time as the cortical development at the center of Sombrun's

14 Corine Sombrun, op. cit., pp. 313-315

theory. The human brain is divided down the middle into two halves or "hemispheres" as they're called, the right brain and the left brain, joined by a thick rope of neurons called the corpus callosum. In late infancy or early childhood, the primary locus of consciousness shifts from the right brain to the left brain.[15]

The relationship between the hemispheres is highly complicated. Each functions somewhat differently and has somewhat different functions.

> Hemispheric specialization, also referred to as cerebral dominance or lateralization of function, is a defining characteristic of the organization of the human brain. This specialization is relative, however, because with a few exceptions, both hemispheres can process most all types of information, although they do so in fundamentally different manners. The right hemisphere excels at more holistic and coarse processing of information, whereas the left excels at more analytic and fine-grained processing of information.[16]

Books have been written about the distinction and interplay between hemispheres in the human brain. Their differences, and the way they work together, are fascinating. They both receive the same sensory input, but they do different things with it. They look at the world through greatly different lenses. For example, although they receive basically similar optical data, the right brain from the left eye and the left brain from the right eye,

> The right brain perceives the longer wavelengths of light. As a result, the visual perception of our right mind is somewhat

15 Chiron C, Jambaque I, Nabbout R, Lounes R, Syrota A, Dulac O. The right brain hemisphere is dominant in human infants. Brain. 1997 Jun;120 (Pt 6):1057-65. doi: 10.1093/brain/120.6.1057. PMID:9217688.
16 M.T. Banich, "Hemispheric Specialization and Cognition" in *Encyclopedia of Neuroscience* (Academic Press 2009)

> blended or softened. This lack of edge perception enables it to focus on the bigger picture of how things relate to one another . . . In contrast, our left brain perceives the shorter wavelengths of light, increasing its ability to clearly delineate sharp boundaries. As a result, our left mind is biologically adept at identifying separation lines between adjacent entities.[17]

Language is mainly a left-brain function. The left brain is associated with analytic, abstract thought. The right brain is associated with feelings of connectedness to the world and nonlinguistic reasoning.

This division of labor has results that you may not expect. In one study, psychiatric patients were subjected to electroconvulsive therapy. In some, it suppressed the left hemisphere, in others the right. While recovering, they were asked to solve logic problems:

> While the right hemisphere was suppressed, syllogisms were usually solved by theoretical, deductive reasoning even when the factual answer was known a priori, the premises were obviously false and the conclusions were absurd. While their left hemisphere was suppressed, the same subjects applied their prior knowledge; if the syllogism content was unfamiliar or false, they refused to answer. We postulate a left-hemisphere mechanism capable of decontextualized mental operations and a right-hemisphere mechanism, the operation of which is context-bound and incapable of abstraction. We show that each hemisphere tends to over-extend its perspective on the problem and that in the intact brain they both contribute to an extent that depends on the characteristics of the problem at hand.[18]

---

17 Jill Bolte Taylor, *My Stroke of Insight* (Viking 2008), p. 143

18 Deglin VL, Kinsbourne M. Divergent thinking styles of the hemispheres: how syllogisms are solved during transitory hemisphere suppression. Brain Cogn. 1996 Aug;31(3):285-307. DOI: 10.1006/brcg.1996.0048. PMID: 8812011

Another way of saying it might be that the left hemisphere tends to reason in the air, while the right hemisphere sticks to the facts, Ma'am, and they collaborate to come up with appropriate solutions.

It made sense to me that the infant uses the right brain to develop a holistic, dynamic, relational understanding of the world it has landed in, closely bound to its factual circumstances, continuing to do so for as long as it can rely on caregivers for its basic needs. Then, about the age when human children start to become physically competent and increasingly responsible for their own survival, the right brain hands over (so to speak) the quotidian reins to the detail-and-planning-oriented left brain. But the right brain doesn't just go away, inhibited or suppressed by the left brain's advent. It keeps working as it always has, but as it were in the background, integrating data into a constantly evolving, constantly refined comprehension of the world's relationships and dynamics, that undergirds and occasionally, when needed or elicited, intrudes into the left brain's ordinary consciousness as an inspiration or aperçu, or even takes over temporarily from ordinary consciousness as a trance state.

All this now acquired renewed relevance to my situation, in two ways.

First, through Corine Sombrun. Towards the end of 2021, Samara had sent me a link to a video of Sombrun giving a public talk about shamanism. She had been working as a reporter for the BBC in Mongolia when the sound of a shamanic drum had thrown her involuntarily into a shamanic trance. A shaman, or udgan as they are known in Mongolia, had witnessed this and invited Sombrun to apprentice. Over the next eight years, Sombrun traveled regularly to Mongolia for training. She achieved the status of udgan, the first Westerner to do so. Later, she developed the ability to enter trance at will, without the use of drugs or external stimuli such as music. She also developed the desire to bring Western science to bear on the many questions and problems posed by shamanic trance.

Using several methods of brain imaging, scientists observed Sombrun in both her normal and trance states.[19] They also obtained from her written descriptions of what she experienced while in trance. (Fascinating reading in themselves. I found them reassuringly validating as to my own experience.) The scientists compared the data thus obtained to a "bank of previously investigated control groups of normal, schizophrenic, manic, and depressed dextral female subjects."

A frequent trope of earlier scholarship on shamanism had been that it is akin to mental illness, or possibly a means by which "primitive" communities provide socially acceptable employment for the mentally ill. (There's some irony in this latter theory, given "advanced" and "civilized" societies' general failure or refusal to grant any useful, let alone respected roles to such persons.) Although similarities were observed between Sombrun's trance-state readings and those of pathological states in the controls, the scientists observed that in shamanic trance,

> the corresponding electrophysiological changes are limited to the trance condition and to a specific band frequency, the subject maintaining the capacity to return to her normal state at will. This capacity for voluntary induction and termination of seemingly pathological brain states coupled with the availability of the internally derived trance

---

19 Pierre Flor-Henry, Yakov Shapiro & Corine Sombrun (2017) Brain changes during a shamanic trance: Altered modes of consciousness, hemispheric laterality, and systemic psychobiology, Cogent Psychology, 4:1, 1313522, DOI: 10.1080/23311908.2017.1313522

> information for subsequent analytical processing is the defining characteristic of functional trance states and [shamanic states of consciousness], which distinguishes them from psychopathology.

But I have been withholding the lede. The scientists' central conclusion was this:

> Our findings point at a unified clinical model of altered state experiences based on a shift from the left hemisphere-dominant, verbally based, serial mode of information processing in normative conscious awareness to right hemisphere-dominant, somatosensory-based, parallel mode of information processing in [altered consciousness] states.

Trance shifts consciousness back into the right brain.

May we pause here for a poem?

In other times, everything
spoke to us. I
rounded up and parsed
the utterances of parsley,
pigs, periwinkles, parrots, and
planets, securing their sense.
I chased such data, tireless
as a border collie
gathering sheep into flocks:
spotted ones here, black ones
there, white set aside.

I fell into
dissection and analysis. I
forgot the chicken bones
deep in the pocket

of my lab coat, that I
sometimes fingered thoughtlessly.
Had I remembered

how to throw them
just so they fell
forming the world's letters,
a script I'd known
to read wherever I found it
before my eyes
had strayed from its
ambiguities to fix upon
a harshly different light,
I could have saved
us so much grief.

38.

Thinking about the hemispheric shift that the neuroscientists had observed in Sombrun's brain during trance, it struck me that another, developmental shift in hemispheric activity might be salient to my own situation: the transitional period at the end of infancy when the prefrontal cortex comes into its own and the right brain turns over to the left its place at the helm.

I thought about the "terrible twos." A radical, involuntary shift in consciousness from relatively peaceful connectedness with one's human and physical environment to an ever more individuated, relatively alienated sense of agency, would be disorienting, frightening, and exciting, simultaneously evoking feelings of helplessness and of power. How else could a person be expected to react, other than with labile moods, tantrums, and erratic, out-of-control behavior?

Layer onto that the coincidence that, right about when my brain was beginning such changes, my mother had become so ill that she temporarily had to hand over care of me to my grandmother. Just when my scheme of things was most in flux, a strong sense of wrongness would have attached to this woman, this interloper as I would have perceived her, this violation of the world order that I had been assembling since birth. That source of all good and warmth, whom I would know later as my mother, had largely disappeared or been displaced. Where she had been was tension, sadness, and a demanding strangeness.

The narrative of child sexual abuse that had emerged in Dr. Rossel's office was consistent with themes prominent in the cultural atmosphere of the time, the 1980s. It reasonably seemed to account for, without quite explaining, much in me that I perceived as problematic. Dr. Rossel, whom I had good reason to trust, had accepted it as more than a working hypothesis. With his help, I had avoided the evil I then feared, that my complicated feelings about parenthood would cause me to become abusive. All the more mysterious, then, my grandmother's powerful, unexpected reappearance more than thirty years later, in trance, after therapy had done all it could to lay her to rest.

I could conclude only that my understanding of our relationship and of its effects upon me was flawed. I had believed that my grandmother had touched me inappropriately. Now, I suspected that this theory was flawed. Challenged by the robed woman to accept her love, I had begun by admitting that my strong belief as to what had happened, to which I had adhered for three decades, rested on shaky evidentiary grounds. I confessed, "I don't really know what took place."

I had received my grandmother's testimony. Set aside the question whether I had received this information from some entity independent of me and properly identifiable with the grandmother I had known in life, or from some sector of my brain that unconsciously retained memories of the time in question and now was reporting them to me through symbolic means. Set aside the reliability of my informant; I had no cause to question it. Her testimony was that she did not know what had happened. The symbolism was precisely expressive: the robed woman had hugged me affectionately; she had offered me her robes as a gesture of protection and comfort; I had recoiled reflexively.

I now felt that I knew only one thing for certain. Under the conditions extant at that time, I would have perceived any intimate touch of my grandmother's, no matter how it was intended, for example, all that was involved with cleaning me while changing diapers, as wrong, a violation.

I had moved through suspicion and aversion to desire for understanding; from there to compassion, happiness, and relief; then to sadness at the loss of the intimacy that might have been; and in the end, to acceptance several times over.

Business concluded, a clink of the glass,
your face among the bubbles
rising through straw-pale liquid,
piercing the surface, and pop! gone.

39. February 4, 2022

Being nothing if not persevering, I returned to the workbook and announced my intention to visit the Lower World and talk with my Guardian Spirit.

As the trance slowly builds, my toes twitch. I notice this because Corine Sombrun's technique of auto-induced trance uses such physical cues as triggers. I am nowhere near that level of proficiency, but someday I'd like to get there.

Down a long, twisty, dark tunnel, I come to hints of the swamp, the spiky, drowned trees reflected in the water, looking as if they are growing upside down. Then, I am flying among the steep, forested mountains. Their deep, vee-shaped valleys through which wriggle lakes and streams remind me of the High Peaks area in the Adirondacks. I'm about a hundred feet up. Lots of mist and fog crawl over the landscape, so I get only a glimpse before anything below is obscured.

A few, small faces quickly come and go. One, larger than the rest, wears a scary, devilish expression. I look at it, and it disappears.

For a while, I look down from a great height onto a large expanse of rounded treetops packed densely together, like olive-green cauliflower florets, a forest on relatively level ground. No Guardian Spirit appears.

I have an urge to growl, and do, releasing a long, gravelly rrrrrrrgh *that empties my lungs and is barely audible to me over the drumming. The gasping inhale that follows is much louder, but does not belong to the trance as the growl did.*

Back among the mountain fogs and mists, I ask if anyone is there for me to talk with. "I am," it answers. "Who are you, who am I talking to?" "The Spirit of Fog." "Where is my Guardian Spirit?" "Not here; you're looking in the wrong place." "Where is it, then?" "In the Middle World." This contradicts the workbook, but I'm slowly learning that, to paraphrase Captain Barbossa in Pirates of the Caribbean, *"The workbook is more what you'd call guidelines than actual rules."*

I decide to stay for now in the Lower World, on the chance that I might meet someone or see something interesting, but it's just the same old same old. I ask the Spirit of Fog if there's anything I can do for it, any offering I can make to express my gratitude for its assistance, but it doesn't answer.

40. February 9, 2022

I dreamed about my maternal grandmother for the first time ever, that I can remember:

> *It is a family reunion in Los Angeles. My sister and I are there. My grandmother arrives after us. She is 96 years old, lively and intelligent, a bit tart and humorous in her manner. She is wearing a grey, cotton sundress, printed with a floral motif. Hugs all around. She hugs my sister, then she and I have a long hug. I embrace her short, stocky body. A little after that, she is tired and lies down on the floor to rest. I tell her that I will drive her back to her hotel when she is ready to leave.*

She may have been done with me, but apparently, I was not done with her.

The grandmother I dreamed of was very little like the person I had known in the flesh. In every aspect but one, they were opposites. They both were short. In life, my maternal grandmother was a tiny woman, not stocky at all. She was not a hugger. She would have been 122 years old in 2022. Far from being "lively and intelligent, a bit tart and humorous," she was extremely quiet and retiring. "Quiet" is the first word that comes up, when anyone is asked to describe her. I do recall a shy, tart smile briefly coloring her expression on one occasion, but that was hardly characteristic. In connection with a family history project some fifty years after my grandmother died, I interviewed her only surviving daughter. My aunt, who was in fact herself both sharp and lively, could not say whether her mother had been intelligent.

Dreams and the dreamworld may not be the same thing, but I think they work together. The reference to my sister was significant. Years ago, we had been rather bitterly alienated. After a long time of mutual avoidance, our reconciliation had been sparked by my casual, impulsive use in an email of a private term of affection, a pet name for her from our happier days. Was the dream assigning credit for that impulse to my grandmother's Spirit? A less literal interpretation would be that the spirit of rapprochement in both cases was the same.

41. February 12, 2022

On February 9, I'd been unable to find my Guardian Spirit because, according to the Spirit of Fog (great name for a consultant!), I was looking in the wrong place. Did this mean that I already had found my Guardian Spirit on a previous Journey in the form of Phoebe the Old English sheepdog? I wasn't so sure about Phoebe. She'd failed to appear when I'd tried to visit her, and even in our first encounter she had been uncommunicative, receding slowly away instead of telling me what services we could perform for each other. I hit on the gambit of asking my Guardian Spirit to meet me in the Garden "in whatever form you choose." There, as suggested by the workbook, I would ask whoever showed up to reveal to me my "hidden strengths."

Almost immediately, I am looking through the familiar trees at a sky almost entirely filled with fluffy, white, cotton ball clouds. I move through the trees. Briefly I feel as if a slender body were pressing against mine. Unlike with my grandmother, this is a sexual feeling. I do not get an erection, although I feel as if I am on the verge of it. I see a long, dark, twisty tunnel. I could go there, but I don't, because I perceive that this somewhat vaginal opening leads to the Lower World and I want to stay in the Middle World. The sexual feeling goes away.

I am in a house. No lights are on, but it isn't dark. It's like being inside on a somewhat overcast day. I wander through the house for a long time, allowing the dreamworld to direct my movements. It's a big house. Doors, windows, halls, a washer/dryer, cabinets in a big, open, farmhouse style kitchen. There's a lot of stuff in here. A green bucket. On a basement wall is a large corkboard with clippings and pictures and a map pinned to it. File cabinets.

"Where is my Guardian Spirit?"

"Upstairs."

I direct my path upstairs. The vision fades to a screen door about six feet in front of me. Beyond the door I see green vegetation and sunlight. I take control of my movement and approach the door. Bands of dark mist pass rhythmically between me and it. I keep moving. I am at the door.

I must have passed through the door, but instead of green vegetation and sunlight I am in darkness among rapidly shifting blobs of color. A few of them contain faces. One is like a child's cartoon drawing of a long, oval, female face with long, wavy hair. I think I know who this is. "Vic?" I ask.

"Yes," she says.

"Are you my Guardian Spirit?"

"Yes."

I feel a chill, as if scared, but instead of jerking away from what I am experiencing, as I have in the past when this sensation has occurred, I stick with it. The chill fills my whole body. My body feels heavy.

Images of shattered things, a broken gear wheel, blood.

Vic, now invisible and not responding to questions, leads me into a clear, rich blackness, deeper and deeper, among bursts of color and through circular dazzles of light, scintillating like fireworks or a scotoma. I think, what is she showing me, where is she taking me? Into the universe in which I am. That's a verbal paraphrase of what she tells me wordlessly. It conveys the sense of dissolving or melting upon death into the cosmos, into the galaxies, stars, interstellar dust and void.

I am beginning to feel as if, despite Vic's affirmation, I have no Guardian Spirit, if that's possible; or am I somehow unable to make contact? I wonder, should I ask for help from Wendy?[20]

A small patch opens in the middle of my field of vision, a patch of mid-day sky, fully overcast with pebbly, light

20 At this moment, according to the time stamp, Wendy Halley was emailing me about scheduling our next appointment.

grey cloud. I hold my gaze steady on it. The patch expands until it is all I see. This persists, although the vision is not entirely stable; sometimes it seems as if I were looking not at the sky but at a video of an old photograph of the sky that has been a bit scratched or torn and taped together. "Who is here?" I ask. "The Sky," it answers. "Are you my Guardian Spirit?"

"Yes."

"What are my hidden strengths?"

"Breadth . . . depth."

With this utterly unexpected answer comes conviction that at last the true Guardian Spirit has appeared. I ask, "What service will you do for me?"

Its answer, like Vic's, is on the borderline of verbal. The word "shelter" comes closest, with the added sense of "enfold you, incorporate you, take you in, absorb you."

I ask, "What can I do for you?"

"Incense, add to me the sweetness of incense." Then the patch slowly closes, like an iris fade-out in an old movie.

After this, there are some more colors and enigmatic images, a couple of which are vivid at the time but will dissipate from memory. A little later, the Journey ends.

Victoria Carter had been my first love. In our mid-teens, we met in 1967 at an American school in Florence, Italy, where our families had taken us. Her blonde hair was straight, not wavy, but otherwise her Spirit looked like her. We trembled on the brink of sex but did not go there, mostly because I wasn't ready. After the school year had ended and we both had returned home, me to Buffalo, New York, and Vic to California, we kept in touch with frequent letters, hoping to find a way to get together again. Our plans came to nothing. She died in a car crash in 1969.

42. February 25, 2022

A small, dark cabin, like a log cabin seen from the side: a box with a triangle on top, and two small windows. Is that Phoebe I glimpse?

The phone rang, interrupting. I set the audio track back to the beginning, and started the Journey over. As I approached trance, the instep of my left foot repeatedly threatened to cramp.

A house plant, some sort of succulent, in a pot on a windowsill. A glimpse of an animal's snout, I think it's Badger's. Trees against the sky.

"Guardian Spirit, are you present?"

"Yes."

"Please take me to the Reflecting Pool and show me what my life would be like if the ice in my boundary stream were melted." (This is the workbook's next assignment. As with the "Guardian Animal Spirit," it's assumed that the Spirits will know what and where the Reflecting Pool is, even if I don't.)

Rapid progress through the woods, looking up at treetops whipping past against a bright blue sky. The trees are fully leafed out.

I'm looking at the sky, without the intervening foliage. It is covered by a light, high-level haze, just diminishing its blueness. I sense I am not seeing the sky directly. I see it clearly, but there is a sort of shimmer and sheen to it. This must be the Reflecting Pool. The sky is reflected in it. The image is steady. Sometimes dark blobs or bright colors or inchoate images burst through it or encroach upon it or pass over it, but the sky remains. I ask again, "You are my Guardian Spirit?"

"Yes."

One or two of the images that very briefly appear over the reflection in the pool have a hint of sex—is that a large, erect-nippled breast? a slender woman's naked, small-breasted torso?—but, as moment adds to moment, I see nothing else identifiable there but the sky. Or, rather, Sky. After a long while, a few circles appear on the surface of the Pool, as if drops of rain or tears have fallen without causing ripples. Just a few.

I ask, "Are you telling me by showing me nothing that the ice can't be melted?"

"Yes." This seems to contradict what I have been taught, that anything in the Garden can be changed, but, as Wendy Halley also teaches, "there are no rules." Maybe the ice is fundamental to me, to the way I am put together.

Later, another possible interpretation dawned on me: except for a little physical intimacy and perhaps some episodes of emotion, including sorrow, of the type that neither outlasts nor has impact beyond its moment (no ripples), nothing would be different.

I ask, "Phoebe, are you here?"

"Yes."

I ask, "Please, may I meet and talk with Vic?"

More time passes. I do not see her, unless that might have been her face, her eye, that rounded smoothness of a shoulder or a buttock or an elbow, emerging and then dissolving so fleetingly, but as the drum's rhythm is just about to signal the Journey's end, and then continuing through those few closing, halting measures, I have a sense in my mouth and lips of being kissed, a cool, refreshing kiss like water, and the words "Goodbye, my love" come to me.

I returned to my body and a quiet, calm sadness.

43. March 6, 2022

Staying with the workbook, I chose to meet my Guardian Spirit in the Garden and ascend together to the Upper World to see what that looks like. Out of confused notions that the Upper World must be above the Middle World so how could Sky rise beyond itself, I directed my invitation to the Guardian Spirit using the name "Phoebe." Even after so many Journeys, I had not yet fully grasped that in the dreamworld there are no rules, "up" and "down" are fungible, and "self" is a concept of extremely limited utility. I hoped that Phoebe and I would fly to the Upper World on the back of the humorous cardinal who had given me an aerial tour of the Garden so long ago. On the other hand, remembering my difficulties in reaching the Lower World, I was not optimistic about the success of this expedition.

> *Several times, I feel that my toes are going to twitch, so I twitch them semi-voluntarily. Almost immediately, I am under the trees, but their tops appear dark and blurry, the way they were in my first Journeys. I recall once again that this results from hurrying, from trying too hard, from pushing at the trance rather than letting it come.*
>
> *A short series of animal faces flashes before me. Those eyes in a white shaggy forehead might be a sheepdog. There's a cat, a fox.*
>
> *Now I see the treetops more clearly, in full leaf against a blue sky. I'm moving through the forest. I don't try to steer myself, trusting that the trance will take me where I need to go. I ask if Phoebe is with me, and get no answer.*
>
> *After a long walk, I approach a very tall pine tree that stands a bit apart from the others. I decide to climb it,*

having seen no sign of the cardinal. I climb slowly, for a very long time, up branch after branch. The branches are more and more wreathed in mist, the higher I go. I keep on climbing. The mist thickens until I am in the clouds, a haze so dense that I know I am making progress upwards only because every so often there is a gap in the milky obscurity through which a limb shows, passing below me, or beyond which I can see the pyramidal apex of this tree slightly less distant than the last time I looked.

At last above the clouds, I reach the tree's uppermost branches. Over my head, right close by, is the hazy, pebbled surface of the Sky that is my Guardian Spirit, a Cloud above the clouds. "Help me to the Upper World," I say.

"Yes," it says.

I may be near the top, but there remains a lot of climbing to do. I climb, climb, climb. Then I am above the tree, once more in the clouds. I keep on seeing patches of light above/ahead, almost breaking through the murk. Each time, I think that must be the Upper World, and pursue it until the clouds close over it.

I am aware at the same time of my physical body, head pressing into the pillow, neck slightly arched, eyes closed but directed upwards, muscles tensing in my shoulders and back, urging me upwards. I consciously relax my muscles several times, breathing into the tension and letting it go, thinking that I don't want to be trying too hard, but each time the tension returns almost as soon as it is released.

I remember Wendy's teaching that one reaches the Upper World after passing through a membrane. I think, this is one thick membrane. I begin to wonder whether the spiritual realm is simply beyond my reach. I remember how difficult the Veil was for me to pass through into the Middle World, at first; now, I don't even notice it. I persevere.

The clouds thin. Through fast-closing cracks I see tree-covered ridgelines, hints of craggy, rocky mountains.

Suddenly, I break through into a world for which I have no vocabulary. It is beyond my capacity to describe. From that alone, I know I am in the Upper World. The colors are deep and rich, and I see with great clarity. The colors merge and meld and shift kaleidoscopically, at first. Part of me worries that this is all I'm going to get, visually. I remember that Wendy says that color blobs are a sign you're pushing the trance. I relax. I think, this is new, I am disoriented, give myself time to learn to read this place, let it come to me.

I see a flat disc of pale, lavender light, surrounded by rings of crystalline pulses of the same pale, lavender light, a bit like the petals of a rose or peony, shifting in shape and among themselves and pulsing outwards in synchrony with the drum. The disc does not pulse or change, just the light flowing through it and its petals. I think, it's a star, and I think, it's like Dante's god.

Something happens. I want to describe the experience by saying, "Now, all around me became a space as deep and black and clear as . . ." but the words "all around" and "space" are meaningless, the "me" nearly so. Spatial orientation is not a concept that applies here, there's no sense of direction, nearly no sense of self; nevertheless, paradoxically, I feel that the entities I am among and I are rising together. They are swirling fronds/beams/strands/curls of light like smoke, if smoke were pure, brilliant, deep, saturated color, graceful as cyclamen petals. We move, although "move" has no meaning here. The one nearest me is a luminous, dark magenta. I realize that these are Spirits, beautiful, peaceful, waving around me like spirals of incense or underwater seaweed. I am seeing Spirits!

The drum calls me back to my body and regular existence, but I do not obey right away. The Spirits don't disappear, and I don't want to leave them. I lie there, watching the Spirits. Already there is that distance between us, that "I" am watching "them."

I descend rapidly through the clouds, then I'm under the Guardian Sky, looking up at it. There's a hole in it, full of varicolored light, and a pattern over the hole, sort of a loose veil of maybe a dozen or so carmine jewels, floating there in the sky below the Sky. It's as if I am looking up through a window as it slowly closes on the Upper World. My body, when I return fully to it, is filled with a sense of solid calm.

Afterwards, I went for a walk. I had gotten accustomed to feeling somewhat spacey for a little while after a Journey, but this was different. As I walked out the door, I told myself that I shouldn't try driving a car right now.

It was a freakishly spring-like, sunny afternoon. Everything that I looked at was alive and fascinating. Reality seemed heightened, similarly to what one might experience on psychedelic drugs or at times of crisis, but benignly different. There was no distortion, no sense of stress. My emotions were placid and cheerful, but not unduly so.

On the corner where my sleepy, residential street intersects busy, four-lane Williston Road, I paused and watched meltwater trickle over the grit and silt beneath the curb. I admired a diamond-shaped medallion of ice on the tousled, dormant grass beside the sidewalk. Across Williston Road,

I walked along East Avenue, its two lanes heavy with traffic, the trees that lined it raising their branches in hosanna. One of them, an ash, appeared to be suffering. It looked perfectly ordinary, but I felt that it radiated the message of its pain. The sensory aspect of "feeling" was prominent here. Although my eyes detected nothing unusual, it was through them that I felt I received the information, through them that I perceived it coming in transparent waves.

I walked over to the tree and laid my hand on its deeply cracked, bossed bark. "Be well. Be well, my friend," I impulsively said aloud. Not a trace of self-consciousness marred my sincerity until I had spoken and been surprised to hear my tone.

I'm not normally like this, but I had just been to heaven.

It took fifteen or twenty minutes more before I started to compose in my head what I was going to write. At that point, I knew I was all the way back in the normal world.

44.

My Sunday brush with heaven was followed the next morning by a whisp of hell. I was sitting on the toilet when a horrible vision seized me. It was of Vladimir Putin hanging by the neck from a lamp post, his severed penis shoved down his throat, while laughing, shabbily dressed men whacked him with broomsticks like a meat piñata.

Fortunately brief, though no less vivid for that, this vision reminded me uncomfortably of the matutinal, raging fantasies that had plagued me daily throughout Trump's tenure in office. Mama Bear may have fortified me against this kind of outrage, but she had not yet immunized me. I called on her and her cubs to come to me now, aware of the irony of seeking strength in a bear's image to resist the helplessness, fear, and horror provoked by Russia's atrocities against Ukraine. In my mind's eye, I saw Mama Bear's protective snarl and the massive swipe of her claws.

On Tuesday, I awoke in a state of unimpaired equanimity. The sorrow with which I greeted *The New York Times'* reportage on that morning's harvest of death was accompanied by sober, implacable anger at its perpetrator-in-chief, in place of the wild, terrorized rage of the day before.

That portion of the brain which gives me poems had fallen silent, for now. I could not find anything to add to what W. H. Auden had written half a century ago, when Russia invaded Czechoslovakia:

August 1968

The Ogre does what ogres can,
Deeds quite impossible for Man,
But one prize is beyond his reach,
The Ogre cannot master Speech.
About a subjugated plain,
Among its desperate and slain,
The Ogre stalks with hands on hips
While drivel gushes from his lips.

Nothing to add, perhaps, except these lines from William Carlos Williams' "Asphodel, That Greeny Flower":

It is difficult
to get the news from poems
yet men die miserably every day
for lack
of what is found there.

45.

At the very end of his Journey through the afterlife, the fourteenth century Florentine poet Dante Alighieri saw something that he identified as God. In the last verses of his *Commedia* (the trilogy on which I modeled *In Dante's Wake*), he described the vision with such lucidity and emotional intensity as to compel even an unbeliever such as myself to accept the reality of his experience. It is one of those supreme moments in literature, when "fiction" and "reality" merge so completely as to render otiose any attempt to separate them. Whatever it was that he'd seen, whatever in his mind's eye he attempted to couple with words, it was God to him.

In my Journey above the Sky above the sky, gazing at the many-petaled, lavender disc, I had associated it with Dante's deity. I was so blown away, so flabbergasted, my thoughts had flown to the only other person I knew who had experienced anything like this, Dante, whom I imagined to have felt similarly awed. In the moment, I had not considered that Dante's depiction bears little resemblance to what was before my eyes.

Although Dante's God, like my mysterious disc, was "living Light," his was multicolored, composed of three circles that were reflected in each other "as rainbow is by rainbow," and somehow this was "painted with our [human] likeness."[21] The main points at which we concurred were that neither of us felt capable of capturing the experience in any language available to him, and that each of us had been granted a vision of Spirit on its supreme level. His visual experience had not been the same as mine, but the dreamworld does not tend to privilege such distinctions. My inkling that the

21 Translations by Robert and Jean Hollander from Dante Alighieri, *Il Paradiso* (Doubleday 2007), Canto XXXIII

pulsing, living, floral light in front of me was associated with Dante's "lofty Light" constituted an indication, according to the dreamworld's magical, associative logic, of some essential connection between them.

However, it wasn't as simple as "lavender disc = medieval Catholic God." The more I thought/felt about it, the less convinced I was that the lavender light itself represented some sort of theophany. "Think/feel" is a term I had learned from *The Bowl of Light*, a memoir by Wendy Halley's teacher Hank Wesselman of his tutelage by and friendship with a Hawaiian shaman, Hale Makua.[22] According to Makua, "think/feel" translates a Polynesian term for mentation that combines cogitation and emotion into one process. It is thus well suited to reflecting on trance.

Part of my reasoning for resisting the light's identification with a deity was aesthetic. Nearly every Journey of mine so far had concluded with a more or less dramatic revelation, springing upon me just before the drum called me home. But the lavender light had appeared before, not as a part of, the prolonged seance with which this Journey had ended. Shouldn't a vision of God be the climactic moment, after which nothing remains to be said or shown? Dante had demonstrated the absolute dramatic rightness of this structure. To the contrary, the lavender light, though astonishing, had not felt like a climax, and what had come afterwards had not felt like a denouement. It was the descent through the clouds, watching the hole in the Sky close, that had felt postcoital, not my spell with the Spirits, which indeed, in retrospect, had partaken something of the timeless ecstasy of orgasm.

---

22 Hank Wesselman, Ph.D., *The Bowl of Light: Ancestral Wisdom From a Hawaiian Shaman* (Sounds True, Inc. 2011)

The power of the vision's impact on this congenital agnostic can be gauged by the fact that I was thinking all of this, and my thoughts were serious and urgent.

A little over a week after visiting the Upper World, I was researching meanings commonly associated with the color lavender, when I was startled to discover an image[23] that depicts, albeit in a static, stylized manner, what I had seen. I stared at it. This, I felt, was the very thing: It was the crown chakra. According to the Tantric branch of Hinduism, in addition to physical organs, human anatomy contains channels that circulate animating "energy" through the body, much as the vascular system circulates blood. These channels run among a number of nodes, or vortices, called chakras. Different sources count differing numbers of chakras; the most common scheme today maps seven of them, ascending along the spine from the coccyx to somewhere atop the head. I am being purposely ambiguous about the position of this last. Some sources place it directly on the head, at the fontanelle. Others place it off the physical body, just above the head. One of the many names for this highest chakra, generally known in the West as the crown chakra, is "Sahasrara," meaning "thousand-petaled." Its emblem is a purple lotus. If you imagine a variety of lavender rhomboids in place of the emblem's lotus petals, fluctuating in luminosity and shade,

23 Image borrowed from Wikipedia, "Sahasrara", https://en.wikipedia.org/wiki/Sahasrara

shifting size and shape and pulsating synchronously at four beats per second, you will get some idea of my vision.

Each chakra is said to express a set of energy potentials. For example, the chakra at the base of the spine is associated with a person's safety and security, basic physical well-being, groundedness. The second chakra, below the level of the navel, has to do with sexuality and creativity. And so on. Sahasrara connects to spirituality. In my understanding, the teachings suppose it to perform a quasi-placental function between the spiritual dimension and the physical plane of our bodily existence.

Tantra teaches that at certain moments in a person's life, a chakra might be "opened" or "activated," fully expressing its potential for the energy flowing through it. Sahasrara's activation would involve feelings of peace, egolessness, connection with other entities, receptivity to subtle energies and communications: for example, captivation by marvel at the mundane, like curbside snowmelt runoff; perception and enjoyment of the rejoicing of trees; compassion for their suffering; and expression to them of that compassion. It might also create a spot of psychic tenderness, extreme sensitivity to the atrocity of war.

I cannot aver that I had never previously seen a description of Sahasrara, its meanings, and its iconography. Although I have no particular memory of it, I am a voracious, omnivorous reader. Much if not all of this information could well have been lodged in my brain long before my March 6 Journey. A parsimonious explanation of the vision could be that my lucid dream called up this imagery from stored data.

No scientifically accepted evidence supports the existence of chakras. The "energy" purportedly spinning in them, of which they are said to be composed, has not been detected by our technology despite a number of attempts. On the other hand, as it is said, "absence of evidence is not evidence of absence." A cautious agnosticism might be called for.

I was not satisfied that my vision of the lavender light could be explained as merely a somewhat distorted retrieval from memory of literary information. That left too much unaccounted for:

- Why would my American, secular, Jewish brain, receiving instruction in trance from a Polynesian perspective, have selected the Hindu chakra as a focal point?
- Why had I been so surprised to discover the lavender light's Tantric association, days later? If its origin was a recovered memory, you'd think it would not have been startling to find out where it came from, since I'd already have had that knowledge, at least unconsciously. I would have met the news with recognition, not startled shock.
- Where did the climactic sojourn with the Spirits come from? I can safely assert that I had never seen, read, or heard anything like it.
- How to account for the Journey's surprising impact upon my feelings and behavior, once it was over? How could that have resulted from revisiting forgotten data concerning an alien religious tradition to which I never had been particularly attracted?
- Sensations and behaviors like those I'd felt and manifested after the Journey might be associated with the release of certain neurotransmitters, for example, dopamine and oxytocin. And feelings of blissful connectedness are characteristic of right-brain consciousness. But, to identify the neurochemical mechanisms

associated with a psychological, behavioral phenomenon is not the same thing as to understand its causation. Knowledge of internal combustion doesn't tell us much about a car trip.

- Why would lying on my back in a darkened room, listening to a drum with the intent of "visiting" the "Upper World" to "look around," lead to conversing with ash trees?

It was almost enough to make one think that one has a luminous, purple lotus floating atop one's head, through which one is tethered to a world of ethereal, fiery cyclamens. How one might be able to see such a thing without a mirror, I had no idea.

I hear the psalmist, faintly, as if from a
distance measured by hundreds of thousands of
days of weary travel by foot,
days afoot as long as years.
He stomps and hollers unembarrassed
in the public square his bawls of
praise and submission, awe and fear,
gratitude for the gift of everything,
desperate pleas for this and that,
casting his words to the kingliest ears
in his world of kingdoms. The distance
flattens his tunes. Is he banging a drum?

46. March 25, 2022

All that frantic intellection covered my inner turbulence like a crust of ice over a river. I performed what had become my pre-Journey ritual in a barely acknowledged state of nervousness and expectation. I blew my shofar, savoring the high, slightly quavering call that I sent out, I like to imagine, across the Worlds to summon my Spirit Helpers. I thanked Badger, Mama Bear and her cubs, Guardian Spirit Sky, and other Helpers known and unknown. All this in the service of composing my mind so as to enter the trance and Journey effectively. I smiled to myself. I took my smile as a sign of relaxation: look, I'm smiling!

Following the workbook, I invited Sky to meet me in the Garden and to accompany me to the Upper World to meet my "Spiritual Teacher." In addition to "Spiritual Teacher," I used the Hawaiian word 'Aumakua, which in one of its meanings is a loose synonym for the term Wendy Halley had used. 'Aumakua also connotes "Oversoul," "ancestor," and the component of a person's being that is said to exist beyond mortality and to absorb the fruits of each of that person's reincarnations.

I had learned this word from Hank Wesselman's book, *The Bowl of Light*. I liked the weight and density of meaning enwebbing the concept of 'Aumakua as a central component of the highly complex, Polynesian spirituality Wesselman describes. I liked the feel of the word in my mouth. By comparison, "Spiritual Teacher," although accessible to a Western reader, felt thin, evocative of an authority imparting instruction. One of Wesselman's aphorisms, "the day of the guru is over," summed up my attitude nicely. This is not to imply that a teacher such as Wendy Halley was unimportant to me. Far from it! But "'Aumakua" expresses a far more intimate relationship. In its thickness, its heft, it felt congruent with what I had experienced so powerfully in my last Journey.

Terminology is so powerful, and can be so difficult! To step for a moment outside the chronological narrative, I eventually became uncomfortable with my use of 'Aumakua which could seem to lay claim to a closer relationship to Hawaiian spirituality than I in fact possess. Fortunately, there is a roughly parallel term in Jewish mysticism, a tradition within my general cultural heritage. That word is Neshama. I will use it in the remainder of this book, mindful that "a rose is a rose is a rose."

On some level, terminology also is beside the point. As Corine Sombrun's teacher in Mongolia had told her upon being requested for some specific instruction about Journeying, "The Spirits will teach you."

In retrospect, it seems significant that I forgot to put on the beaded necklace I had been accustomed to wearing while Journeying. When stressed, I tend to forget things. I was in plenty of stress about this, my first attempt to return to the Upper World. My sense of identity and control had been seriously shaken by the feeling of literal selflessness that had overcome me there, in The Right Place From Which One Never Would Want To Leave. Even after I had bowed to necessity and left there, the accustomed contours of my selfhood had been challenged again by an extraordinarily heightened sensitivity to and connection with the world to which I had returned. Although my strong talent for apparent equanimity, for tamping down emotional extremes, cushioned me now almost to the point of numbness—look, I'm smiling!—beneath conscious awareness I was torn between polarities of terror and bliss.

Somehow, I make it to the Garden, judging by the treetops I see in flashes above me. I keep on telling myself I have to find the Big Tree, to climb through the clouds, in short, to repeat the procedural sequence of the previous Journey.

I don't make it out of the Garden. I don't see the Big Tree, although a couple of times I almost fool myself into thinking I am climbing it. Towards the end of the Journey, I see Sky. He is more overcast than usual. Instead of the pebbly, translucent, high-level haze I've seen on previous occasions, he is covered with purplish clouds. The clouds several times form an upside-down funnel, like an inverted, motionless tornado, narrowing into a sort of cloud tunnel pointing upwards. I do not have the presence of mind to recognize the possibility, dimly felt in the moment but only afterwards raised into consciousness, that Sky is trying to help me, to offer me a route to the Upper World, just as I have asked him to do.

47. April 1, 2022

I woke from a good night's sleep feeling refreshed and energetic, enjoyed a light breakfast of granola and goat's milk and my usual mega-mug of black coffee, read the day's headlines in *The New York Times*, and listened on the radio to the BBC World Service. All of which, topped off by fifteen minutes of meditation, comprised my weekday morning routine. (Retirement is grand!) After which, I felt surprisingly unmotivated. There were plenty of things to do, but I could not summon the will to do any of them. I stared out the kitchen window at the drab, rainy, 45-degree weather for half an hour, reviewing all the activities on hand, feeling heavy and paralyzed.

I had been planning to Journey today, but every time I thought of it, I wanted to put it off until after lunch. At least my mind was giving it a time frame. I felt no impulse to do any of the other things I thought I might be doing, any time in the immediately foreseeable future. But lunchtime was another half an hour off. Plenty of time for a Journey. Maybe, I thought, my will to do anything else was so completely absent because this was what I needed most to do.

Rather than spend another thirty minutes staring at drizzle, I tore myself away from the window and pulled together my ritual paraphernalia. My tone on the shofar today was particularly high and sweet. I invoked my Helpers both known and unknown, and particularly asked Guardian Spirit Sky's assistance in Journeying from the Garden to the Upper World to meet my Neshama. Then, deliberately closing my mind to expectations, I laid down and started the music.

So, looking at the usual treetops, they're very blurry at first, then they come into focus, but the images are sporadic and fragmented and occupy only small fractions of the field of vision.

I twitch my toes, or my toes twitch, toeing the line between voluntary and involuntary motion.

I am seeing shapes and surfaces that seem to be the interior of a building. Right ahead there's a dark, red door. I could go through. I shy away from it. I want to be outside, don't I, to climb up to the Upper World? No sooner do I think this, than I'm outside. Quickly, I realize on some near-the-surface level that I have declined to go in the direction the Journey wants to take me, that I have seized control rather than let it develop freely.

Moving through the woods, I look for the Big Tree, but I don't see it. It gets very misty and hazy, and I keep looking for signs that I am rising through the foliage, not trusting my lack of any feeling of ascent, but anyway, there are none.

A purplish, cloudy sky opens in the center of my field of vision. I concentrate on maintaining sight of it, thinking this is not just sky, it may be Sky, but although I look up into it for a while, I receive no communication from it and see no cloud-funnels opening upwards.

The mist and haze clear, the sky dissolves to something sharply focused and full of color. I think, perhaps I am entering the Upper World, somehow, and like my last time there, maybe it will just take a little while for me to become oriented enough to it to derive some meaning from it.

There's a brief, startlingly vivid, microscopically detailed, close-up view of a tiny twig—a smooth, round, green shoot of new, woody growth. A bud spikes out from the end of it.

Quick glimpses of parts of metallic, spaceship-like objects, interspersed with glimpses of treetops above me.

Did I ever leave the Garden?

When my conscious attention returned to my body, I felt tranquil and relaxed. The mental chatter which ordinarily occupies my mind was greatly reduced, and that too contributed to my sense of peacefulness. My lethargy was gone. In its place, a quiet impulsive decisiveness. I wanted to go for a walk. I did not feel spacey, and would have trusted myself to drive a car; but what I wanted to do was to find out if I could recognize the tree to which I had spoken on March 6, and, if so, how it would appear to me now.

Walking down the street, crossing four-lane Williston Road, and retracing my steps along East Avenue, I noticed that I was more responsive than usual to trees in general. A branch or a trunk would catch my eye, and my gaze would be drawn to it reflexively, lingering on the vaguely evocative, nearly expressive forms. Likewise, I was unusually responsive to figures of tan and dun and olive in the bedraggled, limp, as-yet-unrevived grass bordering the sidewalk. But there was nothing distorted or hallucinatory or otherwise heightened about what I was seeing.

I recognized the tree easily from a distance. It would have been hard to miss, because it was the only tree of its type along that stretch of road. I walked up to it, noting small patches of lichen dappling its deeply creased bark. A few new, skinny twiglets, at least one bearing a bud almost too small to see, needled out from the trunk.

I sensed no distress or other emotion emanating from the tree. It looked like a perfectly normal and stolid, young ash, if somewhat scraggly and sparse up top. I felt calm and cheerful. I placed a hand upon the bark. The bark felt warm and alive. It was like touching a friend's arm.

I continued down East Avenue to the end, maybe three quarters of a mile, then turned around and came back. I laid my hand on the tree again, and again felt living warmth. In a spirit of experimentation as I walked the remaining few hundred yards back to my house, I touched my palm to several tree trunks. A maple. A cedar. They felt cool and a bit damp, befitting the weather.

The next morning, shortly after waking, I wondered: what if I'd been quick enough to board one of those spaceships?

48. April 9, 2022

If at first you don't succeed. . .

An urge to twitch builds in my toes. Resisting the impulse to twitch them anticipatorily, I let them twitch on their own.

I am beneath the Garden's treetops. They're dark, as usual. The sky is grey. I am moving. I wonder, why am I always looking up through the trees, rather than ahead where I'm going? I try to level my gaze, but I don't see much that way, so I give up trying to control it.

An animal face appears, grows larger, its eye black and shining, each hair on its muzzle distinct in the superbly subtle grey scale of an Edward Weston photograph. A fox. "Why are you here?" I ask.

"To help you," it answers, then disappears.

I'm inside a building, a house. The outlines of the doors, halls, windows, and furnishings are vague, as if through a lens smeared with Vaseline. I tell myself not to balk at being inside, to go with it. Will I see the red door? I don't. I am going up stairs. I am going up.

There is a jumble of images, most which will escape memory. It includes strange machinery, a twisting cloud tunnel that I enter, going up. Interplanetary space. Planets. Nebulae. Galaxies. Flashes of flying above treetops.

I am in a place of swirling, purple mists for a long time. I wonder whether I am seeing my crown chakra from within it.

I see Sky. I approach Sky, getting higher and higher, nearer and nearer. I feel that I almost could reach out and touch Sky with my hand. Sky is circular, a pancake of cobblestone-like clouds. It does not strike me as peculiar that Sky has an edge. Sky is boiling around the edge, like a pancake on a greased griddle. I veer towards the edge of Sky, pass through it.

Another jumble of images that I mostly won't be able to remember, later. It evolves into a rapid succession of very sharply focused, very distinct domestic interior scenes, all bathed in green light. Among them: a concrete block, basement wall; a wall with a curved orange appliance like a Dustbuster mounted to it; an empty, plastic laundry basket in a corner.

Then, at last, I am in the place for which there are no words. But I'll try. This is unmistakably the Upper World. Images pass before me: an amethyst cube, a deep blue spark, red beads on a red string, all of them Beings of light. I ask if they are Neshama. "No."

I see Sky again, a circle of Sky, translucent pebbly grey, within a green sphere like a seed within its husk, surrounded by a ring of scintillating, pulsing electric blue-white. "Are you Neshama?" No definite answer. It grows larger and larger, explodes or dissipates into a magenta-red-crimson fire flower, revolving and dancing on an invisible stem, an effulgent cyclamen, its petals ceaselessly, gracefully waving, snapping in auroral sheets and fingers of flame. This is Neshama. "Oh my god you are beautiful!" The words pour out of me. I ask, "How can I serve you?"

"Love."

"What service will you do for me?"

"Teach you to love."

The drum signals Journey's end, but I do not return my attention to my body right away. I watch the vision slowly fade into mere afterimages.

After savoring the stillness for a while, I felt an urge to visit my friend the ash tree and see how it was doing. Before going out the door, I paused for a moment to see if I could have a word with the heart-shaped stone I had brought back from Newfoundland. I knew that such behavior was not normal, but I can't say that I felt anything weird about it, either.

The stone resided in my living room, on the makeshift altar before which I liked to perform my daily meditation. Standing unsupported on its broad end, it glowed weakly pink in the dim sunlight that had made it through the day's clouds and my partly shaded windows.

The thought entered my mind that the stone wanted to be turned over, that it was upside down, that it wanted to be stood on its pointed end. This thought felt somewhat like the dialogue I "hear" in trance, that is, although not sensed through my ears, it did not feel like the product of my creative imagination, either. Outside of trance, by the way, I am not in the habit of hearing voices; it never happens. Visualizing a simple, elegant wooden stand I could make, I said aloud, "I can do that."

I felt a mild chill of fear. Was there some inimical Spirit in the stone that I might release by turning it right side up? I never had felt that I knew why the stone had come to me. I recognized these thoughts as odd in themselves, and that it was decidedly odd to be taking them at all seriously.

I picked the stone up, held it before me cradled in my hands. It felt comfortable to my hands, dense and cool. I decided to consider the matter further before making the stand. The stone was four hundred million years old. It could wait.

Into the raw, chilly, recently rainy morning I went. As after my previous encounter with the Upper World, everything seemed luminous and numinous. Everywhere I looked, banal beauty: the shiny bolt holding a lamp post to its concrete plinth; an empty acorn top submerged in a still puddle beneath the wall of the curb; a maple tree, its uplifted bowl of branches drenched in buds, at the extended instant it is about to begin to spray the palest green.

I walked to the ash tree and laid a hand on it. The tactile sensation presented nothing unusual. As far as I could tell, the tree seemed to be doing alright. I did not feel any special connection with it. The twigs projecting out of its trunk's bark seemed thicker and longer, now. Some of them bore buds. A few had the soft, smooth, almost downy appearance of new growth.

49.

The stone I had brought back from Newfoundland was on my mind a lot, the next few days. I wondered whether I should ask Wendy Halley what to do about it. I wondered whether I should Journey and ask Sky, or perhaps I should try to enter into a dialogue with the stone itself. This brought me back full circle, to wondering whether I should schedule a session with Wendy to learn how to initiate such communication. Or maybe the Spirits would teach me. 'Round and 'round it goes. In addition to the procedural issue, and not too far in the background of it, was trepidation at the possibility of encountering an ill-willed or dangerous Spirit. Despite Wendy's assurances to the contrary, I could not dismiss the notion, received from so many sources including traditional shamans, that Here Be Monsters. The probability that any such monsters existed, like all other Spirits, purely as products of my own mentality was not in itself reassuring. As the ancient Roman playwright Terence said, "I am human, nothing is alien to me." I'd had that vision of piñata Putin. Here Be Monsters, indeed.

By Tuesday, April 12, my thoughts had settled somewhat. What, exactly, was I afraid of? The imagery suggested by the stone's physical appearance was that of a heart, a heart that had chosen to be with me. Here, I felt, I was close to the nub of the matter: a heightened caution, bordering on a fear of intimacy, that to some degree was native to me, but exacerbated by such painful life events as my infantile experience of intimate violation, the distant, sudden death of my first love when I was a teenager, and the bewildering, protracted, agonizing collapse of my marriage in my early fifties. To the extent that this caution was an impairment, it needed to be healed at least as much as it needed to be heeded. Intimacy is always dangerous, but that alone is never enough reason to avoid it.

Yes, it was odd to the point of silly to be thinking about intimacy with a stone, even a heart-shaped one from Canada, and almost as odd to be thinking about using a stone as an "intimacy surrogate" for the purpose of healing old wounds that had been suffered in very real-life situations.

But the idea couldn't be so easily dismissed. One reason had to do with my general attitude about "the other," whether that "other" was a strange and unfamiliar belief system, a foreign culture, or another human being. Basically, if you want to know the other, to understand it, you have to take it on its own terms. I was exploring the dreamworld. I had no doubt that in the dreamworld, the stone could speak. I hadn't really accepted the idea that the stone was a conscious entity, independent and apart from whatever I may project onto it, just as I remained agnostic as to the nature of anything else I might meet in trance; but I felt it important, in the service of the larger project, to act as if that could be a serious possibility until my experience could prove otherwise.

Maybe, I thought, it's not so crazy to try to communicate with a rock. If the root assumption of shamanism, as with some modern theoretical physicists, is that consciousness is everywhere and in everything, then, in order to maintain a healthy stance of agnostic honesty, one must entertain the possibility that the traditionals are right, equally with putting them to their proof.

Also, one does not enter these levels of enchantment without becoming to some extent enchanted. As Alan Tormaid Campbell observed, indigenous societies centered upon living shamanic traditions do not recognize the distinction between "animate" and "inanimate." I reluctantly had to admit that for me, too, this distinction had become somewhat elided.

Moreover, the stone was a heart that wanted to be right side up. Who could say no to that? In words that could be the refrain of a country song, I thought, how can your heart be in the right place if it's upside down?

At the same time as my mind fizzed with the fermentation of these thoughts, I was reading another book by Hank Wesselman which Wendy Halley had recommended. It tells a very intense, dramatic story revolving around Wesselman's introduction to visionary trance. Although my apprenticeship was proceeding in a much more voluntary, prosaic, and low-key manner, I saw much of my experience reflected in his. Not least, he had developed an intense, productive relationship with a rock that he had found on the beach. I was encouraged, reading about it.

What finally decided me to go ahead and make a stand to gently hold my stone "upright," was that I noticed faint markings on one of its sides that looked to me like facial features. Fine, but wasn't that a frown I saw, beneath the nose? No, those were the nasolabial folds. Below them was a thin crack, drawing a greenish line in the stone's rusty pink,[24] a

24 The mineral of which my stone and the Tablelands from which it came are mostly composed, peridotite, is green, but it acquires a ruddy patina from oxidation.

line curling upwards, the amused, lopsided, wry smile of a small mouth. Yes, and around that line very faintly bulged two thick lips. I looked again. The face was wholly benevolent and droll.[25]

I would use some butternut wood that two friends had given me from a tree that they had cut down on their property. They were people of whom I was very fond. I took the stone down to my workshop and positioned it against the butternut. Yes, if I used this piece for the base, cutting it into an almond shape and boring a shallow hole in it for the stone's pointed end to rest in, and then cut the other piece into a horned curve like a crescent moon and attached it behind the stone as a cradling backrest, it would look good and it would hold the stone reasonably well without the need for adhesives. Somehow the idea of applying sticky chemicals to the stone felt wrong, as did

25 I cannot resist a digression on the subject of facial recognition. Various regions of the brain in both hemispheres are involved in facial recognition. However, in 2016 "a right hemispheric dominance in face recognition in humans was confirmed, and the face-selective response was found to be largest in the right middle fusiform gyrus." See https://www.frontiersin.org/articles/10.339/fnbeh.2018.00195/full#h10. It makes sense, in terms of human evolution and individual development, that the right brain would play a dominant role in this ability even into adulthood. For our highly social species, one of the first survival skills that an infant would need to acquire during the early period of right brain dominance before left brain functions have fully developed would be the capacity to distinguish those responsible for care and nourishment. From the early months of life, babies display knowledge of whom those persons are. Later, when the left brain becomes the default seat of quotidian consciousness, the right brain does not lose its primacy regarding facial recognition; otherwise, the left brain would have to waste energy and resources on "reinventing the wheel." Many studies have shown that we also continue in later life to possess a marked propensity for interpreting visual data as containing faces, seeing them in clouds and rocks and tree trunks and emojis. It does not seem unreasonable to ask why that ability is not limited to recognizing faces on fellow animals.

the idea of modifying it in any way. As if I had made up my mind about communicating with the stone, I asked it if it approved of this plan. Well, it didn't say yes, but it didn't object, either. Without further ado, I cut the stand components on my band saw and attached them together. A little experimentation showed that the stand worked best, given the stone's irregular shape, when the side adorned with a face was turned to the front.

Having sanded the wood to the lovely, soft sheen you can coax out of butternut, that would nicely set off the stone's roughness, I applied a coat of beeswax-and-tung-oil finish, went back upstairs, and picked up Wesselman's book, turning to where I had left off reading. Now I learned that after he had taken his rock home, he had discerned a face in it.

Enigmatic one
without touching you
I have broken into you
although no deeper than
your scratched and fractured
surface your cockeyed smile
that promises nothing but
betokens benevolence maybe
a wish in this beholder's eye
that what I can't help but
suspect exists in you
exists in you and
what exists in me
exists for you

50.

This dalliance with the rock, I realized later, was part of a process of recovery from contact with the Upper World. Neshama was certainly benevolent—overwhelmingly so; however, exposure to that Spirit and its environs took a lot out of me. It required strength of a kind that I hadn't even known I possessed, prior to climbing there, strength to a degree that was almost beyond me. Engaging with the Newfoundland stone allowed me to continue to explore the dreamworld while stepping back from the supreme heights.

In the same vein, I dived into the literature of present-day shamanism. I read *Spiritwalker*, Hank Wesselman's account of the series of involuntary, spectacular, visionary experiences that had catapulted him from a normal career as an academic anthropologist into a lifelong study of trance. His visions placed him in the body of a man named Nainoa, living five thousand years in the future on the California coast, long after our civilization has disappeared. I enjoyed the book, while reserving judgment as to its literal truth. According to Deuteronomy 18:21, the test of a prophet is whether his or her prediction comes true. By that token, we will be able to evaluate Wesselman's status in a little over five thousand years. What really grabbed me was what Wesselman had to say about his experience of these experiences:

> Nainoa had been alone when I first "arrived," involved in preparations for his walk. In fact, he was alone for the entirety of [this first] "visit," so most of what I learned from him, his world, and his recent history arrived in my mind as disjointed blocks of—to me—completely new information. I absorbed these blocks as if I were transferring the information from one floppy disk to another. The information

> appeared in the form of impressions, feelings, thoughts, opinions, ideas and memories and would suddenly materialize as a series of vignettes in my awareness. Each would "shade off" gradually into the surrounding ground of my own thought-feeling before the next formed. These scenes came rapidly, in sequence, so that I had little time to consider or think about what I was seeing before the next series began. So I tried to absorb them while I was merged with Nainoa, with the intention of recalling them afterward. It was a little like watching television, but the "show" included far more than just visuals and sound.[26]

Yes! That was what it was like for me too. Until this time, I had encountered nothing so true-to-life as this description of what the dreamworld actually felt like and how it presented itself. How validating and refreshing it was, to read this testimony from an acknowledged master of trance, that his experience so closely resembled my own.

In turn, Wesselman's account brought back to mind a passage I had read recently in Corine Sombrun's book *La Diagonale de la Joie*, loosely centered upon her efforts to work with scientists in developing a scientific perspective on trance. Sadly, the book was not available in English, and I had not studied French since high school, so it was slow going. With the help of a good French/English dictionary and Sombrun's clear, entertaining, informal writing style, I had made it through.

Sombrun describes an experiment that she had done with bowls of water in collaboration with Marc Henry, a professor of chemistry, materials science, and physics at the University of Strasbourg. Dr. Henry wanted to see whether he could detect any change in the water that might be attributable as a reaction to Sombrun observing it while in trance.

---

26 Hank Wesselman, *Spiritwalker: Messages From The Future* (Bantam 1996), p. 53

It does not appear that Dr. Henry achieved any conclusive results. Although it would have been spectacular if he had, that was not the aspect of the experiment that most interested me. Here, in my translation, is Sombrun's account of what transpired. Her style of trance involves a more active form of possession by the vision than the passive descent into reverie I was learning to perform:

> "It's a blind test," said Marc. "I am going to put several ramekins of different waters in front of you. They're numbered. You enter a trance before each one of them and you say what you have sensed. Got it? The trances will be filmed."
>
> I look at ramekin number 1, already before me. My nose approaches the bowl, sniffs. Immediate joy. Huge. Strong. It extends through my whole body. Until the sighing sounds of the sea exit my lips. The power of an ocean. Of an enormous wave. A personality begins to speak through my mouth, a protolanguage with Japanese intonations, that no one listening to could understand. Me, I understand. This water is a treasure. It must be preserved, it has an energy, from primordial information and also from such subtle components, expressed through the sounds and gestures I am making. More harmonious than those of a qi gong master. They give me power, a power that I must diffuse away, far away, everywhere. The impression of being a gushing fountain. My mouth blows bubbles, *blblbloblobl o*. Is it a carbonated water? A song begins. I am certain that it is the song of this water. Very stable and powerful. It passes from a low register to a high register without my voice breaking. How am I capable of traversing so many octaves? I see a whale. Very high-pitched sounds. The whale's. Accompanied by very precise, subtle, harmonious gestures. They continue into the silence. My hands make spirals, more spirals, then all is calm. A profound peace takes me over. Simple. I open my eyes. . .
>
> Ramekin number 2 arrives in front of me. Violent reaction of rejection. Scraping noises, I spit, I creak, with gestures of

> shooing away, of cleaning, followed by the cry of a grouse, *tsktsktsktsktsk*, the shrill whistling of an eagle, the snoring of a pig. Then birdcalls, many little birds, I see them looking up, I sniff, I squawk, I am these birds. A ball. There is a ball above the water. I take it between my hands. I must lift it, throw it outside. My fingers move as if cleaning something, sorting things out, scraping something off. Then their movements soften, their gestures become simple, calm, the trance stops. I open my eyes . . .
>
> He puts another ramekin before me. Something brown, tiny, and indefinable occupies the bottom. "That isn't water?" I ask. Marc says, "No, it's a mushroom. Let's go ahead. I won't tell you its name, for sure. What interests me is what the trance is going to tell you . . ."
>
> I look at the ramekin. What are you going to tell me, you? My body withdraws from the mushroom, small noises, I see a tree, immense, of which my hands circle the trunk and climb, climb, up to the sky. A very beautiful sense of grandeur. Then I return to the ground. My nose approaches the earth, sniffs it, while my arms rise, held behind me, like the leaves of a seedling, pushing, pushing. A tiny personage appears. So small, it laughs, it makes me laugh, I lean towards it while emitting grouigroui, I am an ant, as I watch my fingers become antennae, I become the tiny personage, speaking a language in a very-high-pitched voice, very rapidly. And you, who are you? Another tiny personage appears, facing the first. I become both of them, one after another. One tries to calm the other, who has a crazy laugh. The calmer one wants to laugh, but asks the other to be quiet, to be serious, it is very, very funny, the smaller one is a joker, it amuses itself kindly, not at all wickedly. . . I open my eyes. . .[27]

Three very different reactions to three ramekins. Have you guessed what each contained? In ramekin number 1 was filtered seawater. Regarding ramekin number 2, after the trance had ended, Sombrun guessed that it had been filled from a

27 Corine Sombrun, op. cit., pp. 183-187

toilet. Dr. Henry corrected her, "Just bottled water that one can buy in a store. In view of your reaction, I'm not going to tell you the name, and I'm going to stop drinking it henceforth." With ramekin number 3, it turned out, Dr. Henry had played a trick on Sombrun. It contained a mush made of mushroom. She expressed puzzlement that one mushroom could have two personalities. "No, said Marc, as it happens there were two bits of mushroom, a ganoderm and a coriolus. I didn't tell you, to see."

Let's accept Sombrun's testimony at face value, subject to the caveat that the witness is not available for cross-examination. For at least two of the three samples, trance had presented her with specific, pertinent imagery, clearly implying information that was not available to her by normal sensory processes. One might infer that Sombrun's trance perceptions were ontologically grounded, and that this was so by some means other than sight, taste, touch, hearing, or smell.

Clearly, she was operating at a level far above my pay grade. But then there was a related problem, common to us both. If Corine Sombrun were to walk up to you and say, I am a wave, I am the power of an ocean, I am a gushing fountain, I hear whales talking, you might gather that she is referring to something aquatic, but you would not be likely to understand that she was saying she had been looking at a cup of seawater. Likewise, if she were to tell you about a droll interaction between two ants, each of whom she temporarily had become, you might not gather that she had perceived a morsel of undifferentiated brown mush in the bottom of a bowl as being in fact composed of two different fungi mixed together.

I thought, perhaps the problem for shamanic consciousness is not that it doesn't correlate to the world of ordinary consciousness. Sombrun may have demonstrated that it does, or, to speak more precisely, it can. The problem may be that the communications modalities of ordinary consciousness and of trance are far more different from each other than are Basque and Swahili. Even if ordinary consciousness manages to accomplish some sort of translation of the images trance throws at it, it is like a word-for-word rendering by someone with limited linguistic talents who is far from fluent in the vocabulary and syntax and grammar and idiom and literary traditions and cultural practices of the original speaker, who, in any case, has little notion of speaking slowly and accommodating the listener's level of comprehension. *Pace* Ted Andrews, there's no good Trance/Quotidian dictionary. Lacking an immediately obvious objective correlative, it is highly difficult for ordinary consciousness to grasp what the trance mind is talking about. Conversely, the trance mind may be unconcerned with objective correlatives, meanings in the dreamworld being related to an entirely different order of phenomena.

To pose it as an issue of communication may even have been to understate the problem. Since what is expressed through the linguistic medium of ordinary consciousness, on the one hand, and through the laden imagery of trance, on the other, are complementary views of reality, not redundant, in any given instance their congruence may be minimal. Whatever referent they possess in common, it may not be salient for one or the other or even for both of them. On the one hand, we have a ramekin of brown mush. On the other hand, we have a trio of life forces mingling, to each other's and their own considerable amusement. And they're both the same thing. But maybe they're incommensurate.

To cap it all off, this poem came to me. It refers to the lovely city of Dante, where I met Vic. I had revisited Florence a few years ago, after a fifty-year absence. I think, in the poem's loose concatenation of images, it is trying to tell me something about how ordinary consciousness and trance can speak with each other through a single voice:

Nel Cuore della Città

where I erupted age fifteen
fifty-five years ago
here now

drenched in honeyed evening light

flocks of east Asians
bristle with selfie sticks

a fat German guy and his
wife or girlfriend or daughter
queue up for doner kabob

Rumanians, French, English

at the least hint of rain
tall skinny black men
pop out as if from nowhere
hawking cheap umbrellas

there didn't used to be pizza here
except on sheet trays in bars
little rectangular after-school snacks

now storefront signs all over
sport crudely drawn

round red pies and yellow spaghetti tangles

hollowed out movie set theme park

corpse dressed in the clothes it was wearing
coffin full of coins

barely furnished rooms I lived in

German twenty-somethings
party hearty across the courtyard

the dapper little hotelier
in his white suit and snappy white fedora
doesn't care for Arabs
I have just enough Italian
to understand and not to respond

I stand in line three hours
where there were no lines

this dead-end hall
dead Romans' busts commanded
when it was empty and dusty
opens now before it ends

to the side a big attraction
siphons crowds

away from the disregarded regiment

and the cul-de-sac where
poor Laocoön his sons and the
serpent perpetually struggle

51. May 5, 2022

I thanked the Bear family, Badger, Fox, Cardinal, Sky, and all my other Helpers, and asked Fox and the Bear family to meet me in the Garden and assist me in finding out what the Newfoundland rock had to tell me.

Almost immediately, a scrim of bare tree branches. My toes twitch several times. The branches' tracery grows sharper and closer. I approach the Garden. I am there.

Usually, I am looking up through the treetops when I arrive, but this time my sight line is more level. It's night, but I see the woods before me like a sharp etching, a mix of dark trunks with streaks of white birch. Apart from the birch, I can't identify species. There are no leaves on the trees. The ground is pale with snow. It's winter, here.

I am curving through the woods, slowly. A large, dark shadow keeps passing in front of me. I think it must be Fox or Bear. Briefly, I see a large animal face, probably too blunt a snout for Fox, and anyway this animal is big, so it must be Bear. We pass through these relatively sparse woods into a much denser forest. It's almost black under here.

A small, red dot of light floats across the lower right corner of my sight. Some curved, red filaments appear in the center, before me. I feel chills, as if my body wants to be afraid, but I don't feel fear. Something is here. I ask, "Who are you? Are you the rock?"

"Yes."

"Why are you here?"

"I have come for you." The answer, capable of being interpreted as a threat, sets off more chills.

"Why have you come to me?"

"To show you."

"What do you want?"

"To see."

The vision shifts from the snowy, midnight forest to a bright blue sky mottled with puffy, white clouds, then takes me through a series of landscapes with the palette of the Hudson River School and the precipitous, dramatic compositional style of Albert Bierstadt. This goes on for awhile. I begin to wonder what it means. The imagery comes at me thick and fast. Marble columns; ruined statues with strong features and big, square teeth; skeletal remains; skulls; faces of dead people; faces in the clouds and in the sky; cities and skyscrapers viewed from far above them; thick, jagged, black lines that I take for trees silhouetted atop ridges but I'm told they're "the fingers of the clouds;" they reach down like giant talons; tiny, black skyscrapers with red-lit windows; the recurring thought that I am witnessing the deaths of civilizations; a long series of richly furnished interiors with elaborately, intricately patterned, golden wallpapers—not sure if these are rooms in buildings or in caves.

"I don't understand what you're showing me."

"That's not necessary. Just see. You don't need to understand. See."

"Do you have a name?"

"Dennis."

A football-shaped, rock-like object floats by, swathed in clouds. I concentrate on watching it and thereby holding it in my visual field. "My birth," says Dennis. Airplanes; a spherical, blue and white spaceship. Great nebulous things in the sky. Extremely sharply focused glimpses through small windows of visibility that are almost immediately covered by blurry, translucent panes of color, so I haven't time to make out what they are. I think, maybe I am being given a vision just beyond my power to comprehend. I see Sky. Sometimes, as with the rock that Dennis described as "my birth," I can hold my gaze on an object that otherwise would float away or disappear, but it didn't seem to work on these latest vignettes. I hold on to Sky.

I say to Sky, "I don't understand what Dennis is showing me. What is Dennis showing me?" Sky, though definitely present, does not answer.

Maybe what Dennis had overloaded me with, was little more than an overly loquacious explanation of why Dennis had come to my house. Oldsters have a tendency to answer simple questions with a wealth of anecdote and circumstance. By the time they're done, the question may not be simple any more. Four hundred million years or so of age, Dennis is nothing if not an oldster.

Maybe the sense of threat I'd felt regarding Dennis had emanated from the subject matter of his discourse, not from any malevolence of his. Having spoken with him, I didn't feel him to be malevolent. "I have come for you," he had said, with the cheesy, self-parodying, comically melodramatic menace of a bad horror or gangster movie. Remembering the moment, I thought I should call him "Dennis the Menace." I felt that he had been gently mocking me. He wouldn't have been the first Spirit I'd met with a sense of humor. And there was his lopsided, almost-goofy smile.

Indeed, it might be that an individual mammal such as myself would be almost beneath notice for an entity whose existence spanned geologic time. In that case, the second person had been used not in the singular but in the plural, collective sense. Maybe he had come for the "us" of which I am a part. Of the many things that Dennis had showed me, of those I'd recognized, the emphasis had seemed to be on the scenery of the northeastern Appalachians and even more so on the decadence and fall of human civilizations. Well, human tourists flock to see active volcanoes. Might Dennis have been saying that he is a disaster afficionado who had come here for a good view of the fall of America? Watch out for when they start launching spherical spaceships!

My home in Vermont is not exactly at the center of Western civilization, but it is a darn sight closer than Newfoundland, out there on the northern Atlantic periphery. Maybe Dennis had traded a seat in the bleachers for one nearer to the action. When I'd lived in Boston, I'd done the same at Red Sox games.

I had placed Dennis in a nook in my living room. There he sat, on the floor among my meditation-time incense burner, my carving of Mama Bear, her cubs, and a small, wooden sculpture of Kuan Yin, the Chinese goddess of mercy and compassion, that my daughter had given me. Dennis couldn't see much from there, I thought. On the theory that you don't have to take these things literally in order to take them seriously, but it helps as if you can behave as if both were the case, I moved Dennis over to the bay window in the kitchen. Later, at the sink washing dishes, I glanced over at Dennis. On his face, an accident of lighting emphasized a thin, green line, a c-shaped vein that I previously had overlooked. His smile now appeared much broader and even more cubistically lopsided than before.

Yes, it is silly and odd to mount a rather plain lump of rock on a handmade viewing stand in one's front window as a reward for the rock's sense of fun and adventure. But I looked at Dennis and I couldn't help grinning. He piqued my own sense of fun and adventure so that it glowed. Kindred spirits?

52. May 27, 2022

It felt as if my visit with Dennis had marked a caesura in my trance studies, during which I had recovered my "joie de la transe." To renew my sense of direction, I turned to the workbook. I had reached the part of the curriculum labeled "Heal." The first exercise was to "write how you want to use the next section in the workbook to heal or change."

I wrote, "I want to heal the pain of my divorce." Some two decades earlier, over a span of about eighteen months, my marriage of seventeen years had disintegrated. It had not been an unhappy marriage, anyway not overtly, so this came as a puzzlement to both of us. With no basis of betrayal for reproach, and a mutual desire to behave towards one another with the utmost possible honesty and respect, we had been able to salvage enough of the esteem, liking, and affection that had brought us together in the first place, so that after some time and much labor we were able to continue on as the closest of friends. Nevertheless, despite the intervening deaths of both my parents and the attempted suicide of an intimate relative, not to mention my first love's violent death, up to this time, that is, May 2022, I had never undergone anything to match the prolonged pain of that slow separation.

The workbook said to convene a meeting of my Spirit Helpers in my Garden, to ask for their support and guidance.

I am looking across a large clearing at the wall of trees. The light is low, as in late evening, but the trunks opposite me, though about fifty yards distant, are sharply etched. A few stand out as if by tricks of the light, streaks in hues of grey and brown against the shadowy depths behind them.

A hair-thin, metallic red glimmer, and Fox's face is before me. Fox gazes at me with its left eye, a black, brilliantly shiny orb. Another animal also is briefly present, its dark bulk blurry out of the corner of my eye, as if too close to be in focus: not Bear. Badger, perhaps? It goes away.

Fox says, in images not in words, there is a tunnel. It is round, with blue-black walls, and curves gently in this direction and that through occasional, wide caverns. Floating sheets of glossiness from time to time shoot through it. A faint glow shows the shape of the tunnel's opening into the Lower World, where there are strange communities, communities of feeling, of emotion, architectures of feeling and emotion like something out of science fiction. Fox shows me the CN Tower in Toronto, the Space Needle in Seattle, and the floating cities in Star Wars.

"Yes, in this future visit to the Lower World there are no mists and fog, everything is clear to you even if you don't understand it." I'm not sure who's speaking; probably Fox. The Spirit of Fog will have withdrawn.

Now we are moving rapidly under the trees, through the trees. "Where are we going?" I ask.

"To the House."

Mama Bear appears. She tosses her head, shows her fangs, snarls in a performative way, as if to say, look how fierce I can be. "Don't be afraid of entering the House," she says.

Then Sky takes the floor (so to speak). Sky is more heavily overcast than usual, filled with sometimes turbulent, constantly moving clouds. Sky is a large patch in the center of my field of vision, bordered by blackness, but neither the border nor Sky holds a stable shape, they shift and grow and retreat as if pushing, prodding, and probing each other, perhaps struggling with each other, giving here and gaining there, the central patch of Sky expanding irregularly and as irregularly contracting or being partially occluded. Sometimes the border extends a dark arm into Sky. A gap appears in the clouds, or a funnel pointing upwards. The pseudopod falls apart. Its fragments, corroded and lacy, dwindle and are swept up into the gap or funnel, disappearing into light. This happens over and over, for a long time, like a lesson being repeated until I get it. Something is being communicated that I cannot put into words. Sky turns colors, the lavender of the crown chakra, the flaming crimson and magenta of Neshama (but of course duller than that). This, too, goes on for awhile. I repeatedly anticipate that the drumming will signal Journey's end, but it doesn't. It's like I'm being held in class. I am tempted to think that this vision has some reference to Hale Makua's teaching that upon physical death the Mental Soul renders up itself and all its life experiences to Neshama. Sky says, "Learn to love from Neshama," and it's over.

53. June 1, 2022

ever blooming iris petals whip like flame
atop the stem of this body

These lines came to me a few days after the colloquium on seeking healing.

I was finding it difficult to pull together what I had learned into an action plan, a next step. Perhaps the answer was in the workbook. The next exercise, titled "Meeting Your Future Self," set the task of seeking advice from the person I might become after having achieved the intended healing.

Mindful of Wendy Halley's background in psychotherapy, I thought that this exercise smacked less of time travel and more of an invitation to access whatever I might possess of the mental capacity to extrapolate holistically from present circumstances. It was similar to the "Reflecting Pond" Journey. Surely, if it were possible to communicate with an envisioned future self who has been healed of an agony, it made sense to obtain that person's retrospective wisdom on the pursuit of healing before setting out on the project. Such bootstrapping was not alien to my experience of therapy. In my work with Dr. Rossel, some of our most fruitful moments had been based on the premise that I already knew something, I just hadn't realized it yet.

An animal's face. Whose? It is Mama Bear. She disappears. The red, hair-like glint presages Fox. This time, Fox has yellow eyes, like a natural fox, but it is Fox.

Looking up at token treetops; we're in the Garden.

For most of the rest of the Journey, there's little visual content other than a kaleidoscopic mish mash. However:

A tall, slim man, dressed in a white suit, handsome and white-haired as Ted Danson in the television series The Good Place. *For some reason, the sight of him startles me enough to jerk me into a lighter level of trance. Despite our unfortunate lack of physical resemblance, I think he is the future me. Somewhat later, I am startled again by a golden-robed figure, tiny in the distance, seated in a lotus position, descending through clouds; the future me, again. But neither of these visions says anything.*

The clouds evolve into Sky. It is a night sky, just overcast enough to be starless. Something says, "You are healed. Healing does not mean you don't carry pain." Resistant to the proposition that I'm already as healed as I'm going to get, I speculate that this is Sky describing my future self. Sky lightens. Into Sky disappear lacy fragments of blackness, like what I saw on May 27. "Feed the memories to Neshama," something says. It feels like both Sky and my future self are telling me this.

I ask, "How do I feed the memories to Neshama?"

Comes the answer, "By dying. Or through the crown chakra."

54. June 23, 2022

I came to a decision about the next step. Putting together clues from the May 27 Journey, I would go to the Lower World and visit the community of emotions that Fox had told me I'd find there. Having settled upon this course of action, I checked the workbook to see what it would advise. I was amused to find that it prescribed just such a Journey to the "House of Emotions" to follow the meeting with one's future self.

Almost as soon as I close my eyes, I am in the familiar, circular forest clearing.

Mama Bear gives me a lingering, frontal view of her face—or maybe it's one of the cubs; I'm not sure, and I don't think to ask—while Fox's presence is betokened by a glimpse of red, bright as fire, fine as steel wool, close to the ground.

My gaze gradually descends into darkness. I am sinking into the earth. I go down and down into the black earth, which opens into a tunnel. The tunnel twists right and left, leading down.

Skeletal faces form in the unlit air, skull like, with blocky teeth. I think they look like traditional Polynesian sculpture. I ask, "Who are you?"

"Ancestors."

"What do you want?"

"Fear."

"Why?"

"It feeds us."

I do not feel afraid. I say, "I will give you love." They disappear.

Not long after, I pass through a lengthy, winding cavern of jewels and crystals. The cavern is lit by gleaming reflections off their polished surfaces, and by light from within them. They encrust the walls, dangle from the ceiling, rise from the floor in all sorts of configurations, pillars, thrones, statues, monuments, angular mineral formations. "Lend me your power," I say. I feel energy rush into me.

I continue down, past the jewels. The tunnel levels out, then begins to rise. It is reddish in here, undulant and ribbed, intestinal.

At last, a line of dark foliage silhouetted against a bright, steely sky appears before me and rapidly passes beneath me. Now I cannot make sense of my surroundings. Although I suspect I have arrived in the Lower World, I am not sure. Nothing has meaning, for awhile. I keep on expecting to see the huge A-frame that I saw on a previous Journey, but the expectation is disappointed, as expectations generally are, in the dreamworld as in this. At one point there is the briefest flash of a green basement wall, among other bits that almost add up to some sort of architectural whole but never cohere either in themselves or with each other.

Then I am beneath a sky overcast with translucent, light grey clouds as round and closely packed as cobblestones, and I know I am seeing Sky. It dominates but does not entirely occupy my field of vision, within a black border that squirms and squiggles, fluctuates, expands, and contracts.

I see a speck in the sky, or Sky. It grows into a tiny, white oval with one or two black rectangles in it. It grows larger, or perhaps I am getting closer to it. Now I see that it is a building, a cape house perhaps, viewed from above, like an aerial photo. It disappears.

A small hole opens in the clouds. Through it, in the moment before it closes, I see beyond the cloud cover a swirl of brilliant lavender light—the crown chakra? "Your House of Emotion is in the sky," says a voice.

The clouds grow a bit more opaque and commensurately darker.

55.

Although no drugs were involved, my Journeys were not getting any less trippy.

Writing about June 23, I remembered my father's way of referring to extremely bad news, such as someone's terminal illness or death, as having "a black border on it." Sky within its border—a metaphor for life and death? But I suspected that the symbolism of my vision was not so simple, probably encompassing this relationship, but not limited to it. The frame and its contents were constantly in flux. I remembered the lacy bits of the border that previous Journeys had seen Sky consuming and possibly passing on to Neshama. I remembered that Sky had talked about feeding memories to Neshama upon one's death. Clearly, the black border was an image of multiple dimensions and connotations. A complex dynamic had been represented. Keeping the focus where my father had placed it, one implication could be that death, as perceived by the dreamworld mode of consciousness, is not merely the absence of life, rather, they are entities more or less co-equal and continuously engaged with each other in an environment that includes other actors as well.

The Journey had provided much food for thought. What did the Ancestors mean when they said they want to be fed with fear? I had become used to the Spirits' tendency to laconic, cryptic verbal expression. But this seemed oddly ghoulish. Whatever else my actual ancestors may have been, they weren't ghouls.

In a waking spell at 3:00 a.m. on June 24, the thought came that the Ancestors had been harkening back to a far older, more pervasive, deeply seated trauma than that of marital disappointment. The dreamworld's agenda for my healing extended far beyond the pain of divorce, to my epigenetic inheritance of the effects of Jewish history.

I was born to a Jewish family only seven years after the Holocaust. My favorite Jewish holiday, Pesach, despite its message of triumph and liberation, commemorates exile, bondage, and suffering. The Pesach ritual demands of celebrants that they acknowledge all that history, from enslavement in Egypt to Nazi crematoria, as their own. Unlike the white Christian Americans among whom we live, who collectively tend to view every other group as a rival and threat whether or not that is actually the case, Jews do not need to seek out imaginary or hidden enemies. Those who would harm us announce their intentions openly. I was raised from my earliest years to fear anti-Semites and Nazis, and to fight back against them through remembrance of their victims. Fear, in the form of the injunction to always remember, was one of our historic survival skills. We keep faith with the memory of our ancestors by keeping alive the memory of the fears they endured. The Ancestors wanted to be fed with fear because that was what they believed it took for our people to survive.

But I wanted more for my ancestors (or my Ancestors) than the memory of their victimhood, preserved in the amber of their suffering. I wanted them to persist in the world, in whatever modalities we may pass into beyond death, as full human beings, not merely as the downtrodden and murdered; so that their joy, love, creativity, resourcefulness, intelligence, playfulness, resilience, curiosity, perseverance, discipline, and other qualities might not be lost. To accomplish this, I had to accept them in their entirety, mutilated as they might have been in body and spirit, whole despite and including the disfigurements inflicted upon them.

The vision supported and called for yet another level of understanding. The Ancestors had appeared not as Ashkenazi ghetto Jews, which all of them of the past several hundred years undoubtedly had been (barring such storied exceptions as Cossack rapists, and the like); rather, they'd appeared in Polynesian costumes. In the compressed language of imagery, did this allude to my adoption of Hawaiian spiritual traditions? If so, it alluded as well to indigenous, shamanic cultures in general; and through that link, it alluded more specifically to my own involvement with Native Americans. In one of my first jobs out of law school, I had worked for a year and a half at the Boston Indian Council, an intertribal social service and advocacy organization for Native Americans in the Massachusetts capitol. That profound education had given me a sense of the experiential commonalities between my people and the BIC's clients and staff. We all were living in the aftermath of holocausts, of centuries of oppression. Ironically, by clothing their Jewish selves in Polynesian forms, by identifying with the indigenous, my Ancestors were reminding me that a colonized people, as the Jews were for two thousand years, can become colonizers, as is Israel with relation to the Palestinians. They were calling me to seek equal justice for my people, in every sense of the phrase.

The Ancestors' declaration that "fear feeds us" echoed what Sky had said about feeding Neshama my painful memories. As above, so below?

Perhaps it was Mama Bear who emboldened me. So, when the Ancestors had asked me to keep them in the world through fear, I had offered them love instead. And this had transformed their iconography from scary images of death to beautiful, shining jewels, from which I in turn had drawn energy.

what is more fearful than love
what immersion in the world's more total

what loss greater than having it yanked away
what more all-devouring so that

life as you lived it is not life
and you're no longer and never will be
merely you and yet it makes you

slice down to your own core
round and smooth as an avocado pit
from which you tender something green
that's vulnerable to drought and cold

56.

Meeting with Wendy Halley on June 27, we cleared several boulders from my path.

I began by complaining about my difficulty in visiting the Lower World. Although trance always defied expectations, my repeated visions of the Upper World and of my Garden had possessed a predictability and coherence that was largely absent from my Lower World forays. The Upper World was ethereal, timeless, joyous, psychedelically beautiful, and powerful in more or less the same way each time I'd been there. Similarly, the Garden always presented itself as the same woods, with recurring features such as the clearing I tended to land in and the House of Childhood; and visits there usually had a narrative or at least coherent content. But the Lower World had presented itself radically differently to me each time. Often, I hadn't known when or even whether I had arrived there. Confusingly, entities I had been taught I'd meet in the Lower World, such as the Ancestors or a specific ancestor, showed up elsewhere, in the tunnel between worlds, which I felt belonged to the Middle World. And what was my Emotional Dwelling doing in the sky? Houses belong on earth! In contrast to the relative stability of the other Worlds, the Lower World's landscape differed from one visit to the next—where was the swamp I'd first encountered? The fog-and-mist-shrouded lakes and hills? Come to think of it, in my last few Journeys there hadn't been any Lower World landscape at all!

Even allowing for the dreamworld rule that there are no rules, and the dreamworld principle that meaning is as you find it there, I said, in its radical mutability I found the Lower World "confusing and frustrating, unruly, boundaryless, seemingly random."

Wendy used a two-pronged forklift to help me shift this pile of rocks. First, in what at first appeared to be a digression, she asked what poetry is, to me. I said something to the effect that poetry is a way the left brain and the right brain collaborate to make statements about the world that come from the whole person. I said that I liked to use poetic forms because it is a way of getting the normally dominant left brain to concentrate on such tasks as counting syllables or getting the right number of lines in a stanza, thus distracting it just enough so that the normally silent right brain can step forward to contribute images and substance. But there are no rules about what makes a poem. A poem can be about anything. No logic or discursive reason determines the content of a poem. In short, poetry is unruly, boundaryless, and often seemingly random.

In high school literature class, they'd taught us that you

understand poems by deciphering them as if they were written in code: the snake stands for evil and temptation, the thundercloud stands for anger, the seed stands for possibility and new becoming, and so on. But you can kill poetry by listening to it this way. Before the snake is anything else, it is a snake. To understand the image of a snake, you have to consider all of what a snake is, and not just with your verbal intelligence. You have to smell the snake, feel the snake, hear it, watch its tongue flicker as it smells you back, watch it watch you back, feel the ground on its belly. This is not an analytic process, no more than sipping a cup of coffee or making love is an analytic process. I realized that understanding the Lower World demands that I must pay attention to it the way I pay attention to an approaching poem, before it has found its way into words. I must attend to the life within the images, to their interactions among themselves. That is where the words will come from.

That was the first prong: what I hadn't been doing skillfully enough. Wendy then led me to see the second prong: why the relative facility with which I experienced the Upper and Middle Worlds was impaired for me in the Lower.

In the Polynesian shamanic tradition, Wendy reminded me, a human has three Souls: the Body Soul, the Mental Soul, and the Neshama. Each corresponds to one of the three Worlds. The Body Soul is reflected in the Lower World. Emotions belong to the body. Emotions, she emphasized repeatedly, are powerful, messy, often nasty or worse. They are unruly, unbounded, and operate outside reason and logic.

What did it mean, then, that my Body Soul showed me a House of Emotion in the sky? Or, more accurately, in Sky, my Guardian Spirit? Wendy focused on this image, which she said was beautiful. She asked what "sky" signified to me. I talked about its all-inclusiveness, how it sees everything,

everything occurs beneath it—all qualities one would want in a Guardian Spirit, at least I would. I stumbled through some more sentences without coming up with anything that felt satisfying, and finished with the cliché that "emotions can cloud judgment."

With the air of someone pointing out that you can't find your glasses because they're perched on your head, Wendy said, "The sky belongs to the Mental World. Do you tend to experience and process emotions by thinking through them?"

It took me a moment to reply. I said, "In a conversation like this, you can tell when something true has been said because it brings tears to your eyes. You just described my whole life."

We talked about how twentieth century American men (well, white and Jewish American men, anyway) were conditioned to regard emotions as sources of weakness, things to be managed, minimized, suppressed, or shoved aside. We talked about legal education, training one "to think like a lawyer," to categorize and syllogize and analyze, to marshal facts coldly and to privilege verbal reality over all others. We talked about my upbringing as the eldest male child in an academic Jewish family, where intellect was revered and almost the worst thing that could be said of someone was that they were stupid.

I realized again that I had been attempting to read the Lower World the way that I had been taught in high school to read poetry, to wrest meaning from it by force of intellect, reading literature like a mining company engaged in resource extraction. This was neither a winning strategy in the Middle and Upper Worlds, nor in the Lower World. In the Lower World, emotions are not icons to be labeled, objects to be culled for conversion to my desired uses, or characters I might assign to play roles in an allegory, such as "Mr. Puckish Humor" and "Ms. Raving Rage." They are entities fully in and of themselves. If they might not ultimately be autonomous, independent, intelligent, conscious agents, they act as if they might as well be.

To Journey successfully in the Lower World, I would need to change the way I related to it and to its inhabitants, the Emotions. I would need to stop looking down on them, subordinating them to thought's colonizing might, oppressing them. Perhaps to overextend the metaphor, I would have to move towards a more inclusive, democratic mode of consciousness. Did I have to create this commonwealth of equals before I could Journey to the Lower World? Perhaps, I said, I would make that change through the act of Journeying there successfully. In response, Wendy predicted that I would see a rebirth, a new direction, a revitalization of my poetry, if I were to do so. A powerful incentive!

Toward the end of the hour and a half meeting, I said that I was still puzzled by what I'd been shown of my future self. Ted Danson and a gold-robed Buddha—I couldn't make head nor tail of them!

Wendy asked me to describe Danson as I'd seen him in my trance. I haltingly said, "Tall . . . elegant . . . handsome, in a white suit . . . debonair . . ." but none of this carried any meaning. Wendy said that she knew of Danson as the affable barkeep, former baseball player he'd played in the old TV show *Cheers*; was that what I had in mind?

No, I said, the show evoked in my trance was *The Good Place*, in which Danson played a demon from hell, a sort of Satan-in-reverse who leads a small group of spirits in nonviolent rebellion against the rigidly dysfunctional systems governing the afterlife, ultimately creating a new, functional organization based on equity, justice, and balance.

Aha! Wendy pounced on this. She said she thought it was brilliant. She invited me to view the Spirits' depiction of my future self as Danson's reformed demon Michael—the Spirits are nothing if not humorous—in the context of my relationship to the Three Worlds. At present, that relationship was imbalanced, impaired to the point of dysfunction in the Lower World due to disregard and disrespect for its inhabitants, but this could be rectified if I did the work the Spirits had set out for me. And, as if by way of emphasis, I had been given also the image of a golden-robed Buddha floating down from the skies. What greater image of inner balance could there be than the Buddha? Not, of course, that I would become, literally, "the Buddha," whom indeed I'd seen as a tiny figure, far distant—but achieving that balance would move me closer to enlightenment, to realizing my buddha nature.

Writing my summary of the meeting with Wendy took a long time. There was so much to absorb. When I was done, as if to give me a foretaste of the transformation Wendy had predicted, this poem came to me. It came to me in the voice of Fox, as if Fox were speaking to me and I were taking dictation.

Fox says where are your feet
why do you keep cutting them off
do you not wish to touch the ground
to feel the grass between your toes
the pebbles beneath your sole
grass tickles pebbles are hard but
that must hurt
and the trail of blood is messy
you try to walk so lightly
no one can trace you and

hounds can't find you
sniffing and dangling their stupid
tongues between their teeth
but anyone can follow a trail like that
dark and sticky and thick
if you keep doing that
you will get as white and light and
blown away as cottonwood fluff
don't you want to go where
you want to go
keep your feet on
keep your blood inside
to redden your cheeks
and make your tongue flame
then what they will see
will be you
strong alert and wily
not what you left behind
trying to hide
a smelly runway
leading to where you
left the world
red is a good color says Fox
where would I be
without my feet

57. July 6, 2022

The obvious follow-up, it seemed to me, was to convene the brain trust—Fox, Badger, Bear and her cubs, Father Sky, Cardinal, and whoever else might be helpful—to advise me how to bring my Emotional House out of the clouds and down to where I could visit it. I put it that way, not "how to get to the clouds to visit my Emotional House." Nor did I even consider doing what Sky had suggested, that is, going directly to Neshama. I think that Neshama, in its grandeur and power, had me spooked.

Dimly perceived trees are all around me. I remind myself several times not to push the vision, to let it unfold. They fade into a background of dense, deciduous foliage through which only dim, colorless blotches of sky can be seen. This background is out of focus. Sharply in focus is the foreground. The foreground is a flat sheet of transparency, like stretched, filmy plastic wrap, interposed between me and the background. On the foreground play images in shades of black, flat as a movie. The clear foreground images over the distant, fuzzy background produce a strikingly three-dimensional effect.

The images that play on the scrim mostly don't represent anything that I can understand, although occasionally there is a hint of this or that animal, for example, a relatively bright, brownish line that is reminiscent of the brilliant red hairs with which Fox often announces its presence.

I restrain myself from trying to verbalize what I am seeing, and remind myself instead to just take it in.

Throughout the Journey, I am partially successful at this.

Another level of perception unfolds concurrently with the visual, but comes to conscious awareness only with some degree of delay, sometimes breaking full through into the verbal realm only after the Journey is over. Here's another way of putting it. During the Journey, I am aware of the Spirit Helpers' communication almost exclusively through what they are showing me visually. I sense that there is more going on, but I don't know what. The other, ultimately "verbal" aspect of the communication mostly surfaces in my consciousness with a bit of delay behind the "visual." It's important to understand that I have no sense that the information I'm receiving is being imparted through separate verbal and visual tracks. Rather, I feel that I am receiving a unitary flow of data, which my brain processes in these two, complementary formats; due to the manner in which the input is processed, the output formats are not perfectly synchronized. In what follows, I will put "verbal" communication, and information received verbally, in bold.

My Spirit Helpers are talking among themselves. I am privy to but not part of this conference, aware that it is occurring right in front of me but unable to follow what is being said. They come to a consensus and speak to me as with one voice, saying: there is a tunnel through the earth, the one followed on the last Journey. **You should enter the tunnel to the Lower World.** *I glimpse faces like the Polynesian statues.* **You'll find the Ancestors there.** *One or perhaps several Spirits blaze up from among the Ancestors, gloriously robed, projecting feelings of fearsome power and majesty.* **You need to ask the Ancestors, the chiefs among them. They will know how to do what you are asking.** *A sudden clarity and stability of vision* *shows me sharply defined blocks of intense colors, moving about and fitting together like puzzle pieces.* ***They will explain to you clearly what to do.*** *I continue on through the tunnel until I see a circular glow ahead. I exit through it into the Lower World. A jagged line of trees clearly defined against a bright, steely sky passes swiftly beneath me. I am flying over and through a craggy, wooded landscape, familiar from my first visits to the Lower World. I am in the clouds. Once in a while a flying creature, an insect, bat, or bird briefly emerges from the mist. Some of them are scary.* ***This is the House, which you will have reached following the Ancestors' directions.*** *(I wonder, are my Spirit Helpers using clouds to express their inability to show me anything more specific about the interior of the House) or are the flying creatures the House's inhabitants? The clouds part here and there. Through these quickly closing gaps I glimpse the corner of a room, a small round table, and other furniture.*

58. July 30, 2022

I visited the Ancestors and asked them for directions to the House of Emotions. This time, the "playback" was well synchronized.

I'm in the Garden. I've asked my Spirit Helpers to meet me here, before I go down the tunnel to find the Ancestors. My attention is divided between two planes: my body, lying there in my fragrant bedroom, air cool on my bare arms; and the Garden, dim because I am not fully here. The Journey rapidly becomes more vivid as my consciousness shifts into it.

The upward-pointing tracery of treetops evolves into a similarly branching pattern that leads downward. Treetops reflected in water? Roots? Most likely the latter, as the vision grows darker until nothing is visually distinguishable. Okay, I have followed the roots down into the earth.

There's a tunnel. I enter it, moving slowly down it. I am not exactly impatient, but I would like to go faster. I try. Nothing doing. I poke along.

There's a red gleam, the fine fur of Fox just ahead of me. Fox is not exactly leading me ahead, though. It's almost as if Fox is slowing me down. Fox says, "Are you ready for this?"

I say, "I'm ready," although I haven't much of an idea what Fox means by the question. I presume that Fox is hinting that some sort of ordeal or trial is in store. For no reason that I can identify, I feel confident.

Pretty soon, the tunnel widens out into a lightless cavern. It feels huge. Faces show themselves, emerging from the darkness like fish coming to the surface. One face in particular. It is not one of the Polynesian masks. It is a rudimentary indication of a face, hole for a mouth, bump for a nose, bulging circles for eyes, with very little individuality, a generic kindergartner's lump-of-clay kind of face, but I recognize it as an Ancestor. "Please take me to the Ones who can tell me how to visit my Emotional House," I say.

It leads me past other, similar faces. Despite their rudimentary appearance, I feel that each one possesses a separate identity. Some of them evoke twinges of fear, but I don't hesitate, following my leader steadily among them.

I thank the Ancestors for the help they have given and are about to give, and ask them, "What can I give you in thanks?"

They answer, "Your body."

I have to think about this. Are they saying they want to possess me? I don't want that. But then I realize that these are MY ancestors, they live in me already. "You have my body," I say.

This seems to have been the right answer, because right away the first of a series of ridge lines, jagged with trees, passes beneath me. "You must go to the Lower World," the Ancestors are saying. Their advice continues in this vein, an audio-visual presentation. A white-headed, white-face bird with the beak of an eagle flies toward me. "This is the Phoenix. You must call Her to you, and ride Her." White rats gnaw something. "The rats will eat you." I am not sure whether this means that I will be eaten by rats unless I mount the Phoenix, or if it is necessary to be consumed by them first, in order to be able to fly with her. I feel that the Ancestors are saying the latter: You must be eaten by rats. The clouds beneath us open to reveal a heavy, golden door decorated with golden, geometric designs. I try to assign a verbal meaning to the door, and the clouds close over it. I let go, and the clouds part, revealing it more fully. Then I see a very tall, cylindrical, golden tower. "Enter the tower through the golden door, and climb to the top. Look out from the top of the tower, and see what is around you. This is the true Lower World, that you have not seen before." The Phoenix appears beside me, on my right. She looks at me, head slightly tilted to the left. If a raptor can have a benevolent expression, she does. "Ride the Phoenix into the sunset." The sunset is magnificent, a swirl of reds, purples, magentas. As we fly through it, I become aware that the clouds have faces, crudely figured like the Ancestors' faces. "These are the Emotions. Some of them are frightening, but do not be afraid. Face them. Talk with them. You are in the House of Emotions. It is not a place in which the Emotions are contained, it is what they have built out of themselves."

I wonder, am I there, or am I being shown what awaits me, there? Whichever it is, in whatever sense I am bearing witness, I'm among them for a while. Gradually, the cloudy veil thins until there is just the thinnest scrim separating me from—what? I sense overwhelming vastness just beyond, dark and tinged with red. There are things in it, but I can't make them out. A huge, orangish-red sphere. Peace, tranquility, vast spaciousness.

After the drumbeat stopped, I laid there for a few moments, recovering my body. I got up, walked to the kitchen. It was time for lunch. The plan for the day was kimchi pancakes. Assembling the ingredients, I noticed that I was feeling rather queasy. But I also was hungry. I snacked on a slice of bread with cherry preserves, and went ahead with my cooking. I felt hot and sweaty, although it was not a hot day, in fact, it was overcast and mild. I wolfed down a small, dried sausage. I was tired, oddly close to tears. I cooked my kimchijeon, slathered hot sauce on one, ate it rapidly.

Finally, about half an hour after the Journey, with a full stomach, I felt more like my usual self, plus the usual post-Journey spaciness. I wondered whether my odd sensations had anything to do with the Ancestors' request for my body. More likely, I thought, the nausea, craving, hot flash, fatigue, and near-weepiness were the aftereffects in close proximity to powerful emotional turbulence. As if the former and the latter were mutually exclusive alternatives. Was I ready for this, Fox had asked. I had to conclude, just barely.

59.

And what about those rats?

I remembered what had been responsible for turning out the lights in my House of Childhood. If the House of Childhood was part of my psychological inventory, then hadn't I already been gnawed by rats? But those rodents, although white like the ones the Ancestors had shown me just now, were gone, turned to dust. Or so I had been told, on good authority. Granted, in the dreamworld, anything may change from one moment to the next; nothing is confined to a particular state or definition; the language of image is fluid, its vocabulary shifting with context and with whatever aspect of an object is under consideration. This may not be as strange as it seems. In ordinary consciousness, we don't repeat ourselves verbatim every time we speak on a particular topic. We might even contradict ourselves. Why should trance be more consistent? Still, as the King of Siam said to Anna, "It is a puzzlement."

> **Email Message, July 31, 2022, 11:57 a.m.:** Hi, Wendy. I'd like to make an appointment to see you. Since we last met, in June, I've Journeyed twice. You may remember that I was trying to visit my Emotional House, and had found that it was up in the clouds, up in the sky. So, after meeting with you, I convened my Spirit Helpers in my Garden to advise me how to bring the Emotional House down to earth, to where I could visit it. They told me I would have to Journey to ask my Ancestors about that. So, a few weeks later, that's what I did. The Ancestors gave me fairly detailed instructions as to how to visit the House of Emotions. (It includes getting eaten by rats and flying on the back of a Phoenix and giving the Ancestors my body.) They showed me what I would find in the House, and told me what to do there.

Fine. But for about half an hour after that Journey was over, I experienced some physical symptoms—nausea, a hot flash and sweating, food craving, fatigue, weepiness. This was in addition to the usual post-Journey spaciness. There's more to say, but that's the 25 words or less version. I want to follow up on what the Ancestors told me, but I feel as if it's important at this juncture to proceed carefully. So, I'd like to talk with you about all this, and I think I'd like to take you up on your offer to Journey with you drumming.

Email Message, July 31, 2022, 4:42 p.m.: Hi Seth. Sounds like an intense experience. Are you available to meet either Wed, Aug 10th at 3:30pm or Wed, Aug 24 at 3pm?—wendy

Email Message, July 31, 2022, 5:11 p.m.: Thanks for getting back to me so fast—I wasn't expecting to hear from you on a Sunday. Yeah, it was pretty intense. August 10 would be great. I'll send you my notes of the two trips before then.

Fox says, this is real, it really happens.
This isn't just an experiment
going on between your ears,
results you can read about
later after you've had dinner
and a nice cup of tea.
Where do you think you live?
No, really.
Forget "natural" and "supernatural."
There is one world only:
brought you by a body
whose workings and passions
are as unknown to you
as the bottom of the ocean
with its twisty currents

and millions of eyes
going about their business
there in the deep that can't be
bothered to look up at your
small and unimportant brain
paddling and splashing about
on the surface and pretending
it's the first person.
Did you think you can put on
your little mask and flippers,
hold your breath, and dive
among the huge and strange
Powers that sustain you,
observing and disturbing
Their delicate arrangements,
without being changed?

60.

The date appointed for my meeting with Wendy Halley came and went and I didn't see her. Medical events intervened. Earlier that year, my longstanding hypertension had escaped the control of the medications I had been taking, resulting in multiple trips to the emergency room and tinkering with prescriptions and dosages. By the beginning of August, my blood pressure had been stable and satisfactory for several months. But now, the day before I was to meet Wendy, it spiked again. Not to dangerous levels, to be sure, but enough to upset my already precarious emotional equilibrium. I thought that until this medical issue was resolved, I couldn't be psychologically present and mentally focused enough to talk productively about my recent Journeys. I texted Wendy a request to reschedule. My blood pressure returned to normal a few days later.

When Wendy and I met on the morning of August 25, I explained why I had canceled our previous appointment. She asked if I thought the rise in blood pressure had been related to our impending meeting. That possibility had crossed my mind, but I said, "No." Which was a silly thing to say, even though at the moment I believed it. The true answer would have been, "I don't know, but probably. Those last Journeys shook me up. I was anxious and eager to meet with you, and anxious about where that might take me."

That untruth was the first sign that my brain was profoundly at odds with itself, but at the time I failed to recognize it as such. I failed to recognize it at all. I was focused on my reactions to manifestations of the conflict, not on the conflict itself. So I talked about Fox's dilatory behavior and premonitory question, "Are you ready for this?" I spoke of the message about being eaten by rats. I recalled the overwhelming power of the swirling, gusting, gale force, almost faceless entities inhabiting and constituting the House of Emotion—even just being shown them, without actually meeting them, had given me the willies. I said I was troubled by the strange vision of a vast tranquility, and the enormous orange orb I'd seen in it, like a red giant star.

The conversation proceeded in a nonlinear fashion. Throughout, I was off balance. Afterwards, I was unable to reconstruct it sequentially, or to recall all that we had touched upon. It was a conversation that was a journey in itself, full of moments of discovery, adding up to more than the overt content, ramifying beyond our face-to-face meeting.

The prospect of being eaten by rats, even "only" symbolically in the dreamworld, was disturbing, especially now that

I knew how powerfully and immediately trance experiences could carry over into physical, daily reality. It wasn't just a matter of feeling blissed out for a little while and hugging trees. I was afraid of coming back to a body that was ill, vomiting or worse, or to a mind no longer the one I was used to. I expressed the hopeful thought that maybe I'd already been through this ordeal. I reminded Wendy about the rats in the House of Childhood, how their nibbling had put out the lights, how they had turned to dust and were gone. But maybe these were different rats, by whom I now was to be consumed?

"It's a symbol," said Wendy. She said that this kind of thing happens to everyone who explores shamanic consciousness far enough. When Wendy's teacher had revealed to her that this would be the next step in her own progress, she had embraced it eagerly. In the trance, you die, your body is torn apart, you are reconstituted. Wendy used a particular word to describe this process. I was mindful that Mircea Eliade had devoted a whole chapter of his book to it. He had identified it as one of the features of shamanism that appears almost universally across cultures. Birds might peck you to pieces, wild beasts tear you to bits, a cook hack you up with an ax and toss the chunks into a boiling pot for soup. Your bones might be replaced by stones or other magical substances.

Wendy told me that she had been eaten by rats, as I was being called to do. She said that it had taken them a long time to eat her. She had grown impatient, wanting them to get it over and done with. Then a wolf had shown up and finished the job quickly.

I found this both gross and comforting. It was an experience during which one might feel boredom. That's a lot less scary than, say, mortal agony or an uncontrollable plunge into the abyss of insanity. I began to feel relief, a sense of lightness.

Wendy kept a collection of bones on a large breakfront cabinet in the room where we sat. She said she liked bones, inspired by the Sioux medicine man Frank Fools Crow, who spoke of himself and other shamans as "hollow bones," through whom spiritual power flows unimpeded. Flutes can be made of hollow bones. Hollow bones: on the one hand, nothing in the dreamworld is to be taken literally; on the other hand, "hollow bones" is not just a figure of speech and Fools Crow wasn't just employing a metaphor. He meant exactly what he said, even though his words didn't mean the same thing they would to, say, an osteologist.

I kept on using the word "disembodiment" to refer to the process Wendy was talking about. The word she used was more concrete, vivid, and accurate a descriptor. I was aware of the difference, and remarked upon it to her, but I could not hold the word she used in my mind from one second to the next. Something was seized up around that word.

I was afraid of death. Not directly afraid of physical death—not in this context, that is—but of the death of the ego, of losing my self, a prospect which my ego associated with physical death, with "disembodiment." I was literally afraid of losing "my" mind, or more accurately, of my ego becoming ungrounded. I joked about waking up like the QAnon Shaman. I was afraid of ending, of suddenly being no longer me, of having been ejected from "my" body.

"The ego doesn't end," said Wendy. "It changes. You get Ego 2.0."

Wendy prompted me to search for the roots of my fear. Nothing I said in response seemed to lead anywhere.

She asked whether I had experienced a chaotic, overwhelming period in my life. At least three or four possible, truthful answers to this question boiled down to "Yes," but it was as if I knew none of them. "No," I said: I had grown up loved, in a loving, stable family; I was smart, healthy, successful, and cherished; I knew no material want, growing up; all my interests were encouraged. All, only partial truths, as if no darkness ever had touched me.

Focusing on the present, I said that I was comfortable in the world, comfortable in the world's welcome for me. Once again, my mind swept so much under the rug, as if hiding these things from itself: my horrible rage at politics, the UR-trauma of my mother's illness during my toddlerhood, my ingrained feeling that something was wrong with me, my feelings of alienation due to being Jewish in a Christian country and introverted in a culture dominated by extroverts.

"I am blessed with a beautiful ego!" begins a not-very-good poem I wrote in 1990, when I was thirty-eight and entering fatherhood. "My ego is happy with itself," I told Wendy. "It doesn't want change." Here, without knowing it, I had come close to the crux of the matter: the part of my brain that favors abstractions over facts, that dominates the conduct of daily life, was terrified of ceding an inch to its hidden counterpart.

I continued to utter self-contradictions, unaware of doing so. "Self contradiction" is a singularly apt term for what I was experiencing. I said that if I never had encountered the shamanic path, I would have continued to live a perfectly happy and productive life. In the same breath, I acknowledged that lighting the hearth in the House of Childhood had ended a year and a half of the writer's block that had threatened to destroy my identity. Perhaps such moments were indicative of the seams of my ego already beginning to open, like a chrysalis, with shamanism as the unacknowledged line of fracture.

But the toothpaste (to mix metaphors) could not be put back in the tube. I went on: more recently, my Journeying towards the House of Emotions had sparked a new development in my writing, as Wendy had predicted, with the two poems Fox had given me, the first in particular unlike anything I had written before.

"I want to be bigger, more fully alive," I said. Something swelled within me.

A thought struck me, harkening back to an earlier thread of our conversation. All of the women with whom I had been most deeply involved had grown up in emotional chaos. They came from deeply dysfunctional families, and/or their mothers had mental illness, and/or they were mentally ill themselves.

"They manage it for you," said Wendy.

"They have experience with it," I said. I was, again, not conscious that in this moment I acknowledged what I had been so busy denying not long before. But acknowledging it somehow made other things seem more possible.

I leaped to another topic. "Ever since the Ancestors showed me the rats gnawing on my bones, I've known that this was a passage I had to go through," I said, "but how do I approach it? How do I become ready?"

Wendy told me that she had called her Spirit Helpers to make a ceremony of her—what was the word she used? Not "disembodiment."

I latched onto this idea. "Latched onto"—a baby gaining nourishment from its mother—the metaphor is not inappropriate. But something in me still clung to fear. "Yes! That would make the experience more . . . manageable," I said.

Wendy corrected me. The point was not to guide or control the dis-whatever-it-was, but to enlist the Spirit Helpers' strength and support.

I felt clarity and confidence slowly rising in me, warming me, coupled with awareness that the light was not yet entirely above the horizon. "I'll know I'm ready when this feels like something I want to do, instead of medicine I have to take."

We talked about the part of the vision that puzzled me the most, that is, the vast, tranquil place with the giant, red star. Its orangish disc had filled much of my visual field. "It was like I had gone through the House of Emotion and was looking out the screen door in back."

Wendy asked what it reminded me of. Without hesitation, I said that it was reminiscent of visiting the Upper World. It occurred to me that a red giant is a star in the later stages of its evolution, just as I, having turned seventy, had entered the later stages of mine. With Wendy's gentle prodding, I began to understand that the Ancestors had shown me where a successful acquaintance with the House of Emotion would lead me: to Neshama.

I exclaimed, "I can't see any other purpose in life!"

"Well," demurred Wendy, "it might depend on who's talking."

I asked Wendy, "Isn't this initiatory process, whatever you call it, traditionally part of being called to a shaman's vocation?" But I had been clear in my mind from the very beginning that I didn't feel called to be a healer! Nor did I want to be. This was another source of my discomfort. From Eliade and other authorities I had learned that the Spirits may choose you, without much regard to whether or not you like it.

Wendy responded that there are many modes other than healing for employing trance in service of the community. There are lawyers, doctors, engineers, and writers (she emphasized this last) who use shamanic consciousness to further their work. I asked Wendy if there was a community of such people in our area, "like a bar where the shamans hang out?" Not as such, she replied, although groups do come together occasionally. I thought, well, maybe I am moving towards readiness for that, too.

But first, I'd have to be dismembered. That was the word she used.

I am blessed with a beautiful ego!
Like a silvery eel, it slips through gaps
and slides across the rocks.
Muscles shivering down its length
shimmer its silky skin.

It goes on from there.

61. September 18, 2022

At last, I felt convinced—well, mostly convinced—that passing through dismemberment on my way to the House of Emotion would overall be a positive although possibly unpleasant step to take. This wasn't quite the state of desire that I had identified to Wendy as my criterion for readiness, but, well . . . call it a state of determination. Somewhat nervously, I asked Fox, Badger, Mama Bear and the cubs, and Father Sky to meet me in my Garden and support me in my trip to the Lower World to find Phoenix and "ride her to my dismemberment . . . rememberment . . . rebirth . . . closer to Neshama."

Dim branches, grey tracery on grey sky. A long time in this ambiguous place, not sure whether I have reached all the way through the veil to the Garden. Directly overhead, a grey circle of sky surrounded by grey treetops. Maybe a quick flash of red. Could be Fox? A dark eye; whose?

Dark, darker, darker. Am I sinking into the ground, as before? But that time I saw roots and followed them down. Now it is just a deepening blackness. I decide I will find a tunnel.

Soon I am moving more swiftly through the dark, with the sense that I am following a tunnel, winding through the earth, following its twists and turns, sometimes catching a hint of a round wall ahead. Mostly, I can't see anything. The sense of movement is purely kinetic, not based on visual cues. Just ahead, the tunnel forks. This I can see. Which way shall I go? The left branch leaks a bit more light than the right branch, so I go left. Almost immediately, the light is extinguished. Have I made a mistake? But I keep moving on, following the tunnel deeper.

The darkness thickens into an unrelieved, velvety black. I feel that the tunnel has opened around me, that I am in an extensive cavern chamber. Somebody is in here with me. Insubstantial, transparent, a swirl of presence with blank eyes. A ghost? Ghosts plural? "Who is there?"

"Ancestors," comes the reply.

I move through the sparsely populated cavern. I come to something like a throne, with a majestic figure seated upon it. Visually, this information is conveyed in flashes of geometric form and jeweled splendor that last but an instant. I have seen a figure like this before, among the Ancestors. I ask for help finding my way to the Lower World, the Phoenix. "You're not ready," it says.

Unwilling to accept this, I tell myself that it is me projecting my feelings, that is, only my nervousness speaking, not a genuine Spirit voice. I move past the throne, through inchoate blasts of yellow and silver, calling the Phoenix to come to me.

I begin to see the jagged tree-lined ridgetops, the bright steely sky that I associate with the Lower World. But there's something different from previous Journeys, when I passed above them. Now, though, they move across my visual field differently, as if they are above me. I feel as if I am above them and beneath them at the same time.

How am I moving, now? I feel as if I were flying. Am I riding the Phoenix? Have I become the Phoenix? At no time do I see anything indicating her presence, nor does she communicate with me. The feeling of not knowing what is happening, which has nagged at me all through this Journey, sharpens.

I fix my vision on a patch of sky. It slowly expands until it is all I see, and I/we rise through it. I/we fly over a landscape almost entirely obscured by heavy, milky mist. Here and there, single trees stand out in stark relief. The mist takes on lavender colors. There, ahead, a tree marks a flat place. I think, that is where we are going to land. But we don't. We keep on flying. I keep on looking for a place to land. Our head/s turn/s from side to side, looking for something. Looking for rats? . . . and so, on that question, the Journey ends.

I should have listened to the Ancestor. Everything that had happened after I had pushed past the throne was confirmation that I wasn't ready.

I masticated this and that theory as to the source of my unreadiness. Mostly, I thought that my ego had gotten in the way, shoving ahead in a spirit of self-aggrandizement. I had to admit, I'd been congratulating myself on the distinction presumably conferred on me by possessing the almost unique prospect of dismemberment by rats, an honor (as I construed it) shared only by Wendy Halley. I'd been congratulating myself, despite my misgivings, with the notion that a call to dismemberment might indicate a special vocation, a special aptitude. I'd even been toying smugly, out of some obscure sense of competition, with the thought that Samara had not mentioned going through this initiatory ordeal. Ego had goaded me into disregarding the Ancestor's clear evaluation of my unreadiness. If ego wanted me to be ready, then according to ego I must be ready! My ego, that did not want to change, had tried to take charge of the process whereby it would be changed.

Obviously, in a contest between ego and the Spirits, ego loses. If you're not ready for an experience in the dreamworld, I thought, you just don't experience it.

Forgetting that I already had recognized a clear and doable standard, that is, genuinely wanting to be dismembered, I decided to ask the Ancestors how to become ready.

Think, think, think.

62. September 19, 2022

"I call upon my Spirit Helpers for support and, if necessary, assistance in my Journey to the cave of the Ancestors to ask them how do I become ready." Surprised at the depth of yearning in my voice, I repeated, "How do I become ready?" It deepened. I felt near tears. This was coming from a level far beneath cocky self-assurance and self-assertion. It felt like a form of surrender. Again I pleaded, "How do I become ready?"

The trees of the Garden weave their dim, loose basket around me. Spheres of white light flash from time to time around the edges, and a bolt of lightning.

A patch of overcast, night sky appears. Is it Sky? It expands until it is all I see. Lightning bursts across it again. I remember that outdoors, back in the world of ordinary consciousness, which seems very far away, a thunderstorm began just as I was lying down to commence this Journey.

I am stationary. I decide to look for a tunnel. I approach a big pine tree and look down its trunk, seeking to follow its roots into the ground. I envision the split tree with its hollowed bole that I had identified as a route to the Lower World.

After a while of groping in the darkness, I see a spot of glow and move towards it. Uncertainty whether I should be so assertive overcomes me. The glow and motion disappear. I wait a while for things to happen, but they don't. There's a glow again. I follow it. It becomes a tunnel, the familiar tunnel, intestinally recursive. After a shorter walk than I expected, it debouches into velvet blackness. This is not yet the cavern, though. I climb over many rock formations, their blocky outlines just barely visible, big and square as if roughly hewn, the passage squeezing among them. There's a point of grey dead ahead in the center of immense lightlessness.

Now I'm in a cavern. Someone is with me. Or someones. "Who are you?"

No answer. Prickly chills of fear crawl across my scalp. A pair of eyes glints near me—and was that teeth? A giant insect abdomen? A fiery red skull! I keep moving determinedly forward. The fear mounts, then dissipates. I have passed beyond whatever was scaring me.

For the briefest instant, a red hair slices the darkness. Fox?

For another instant, a hint of the color and regal magnificence of the Ancestor who spoke to me the day before. I apologize for my behavior then, and ask, "How do I become ready?"

I am shown by the Ancestors—or perhaps a lone, regal Ancestor is my interlocutor—ragged, tree-topped ridgelines passing over me. "You must go to the Lower World." This continues for a long time, then there's a glimpse of a huge raptor flying toward me. The words that come to me are, "You must call the Phoenix," but I am not sure of the meaning. Maybe I must seek the Phoenix, or I must wait for the Phoenix to find me. And then there's a very long series of shifting colored shapes, flowing into one another, for which I can find no correlatives. I say, "I don't understand what you are showing me, and I ask Fox for help interpreting it, but to no avail. At one point, though, I think I see Fox's head, profiled against a brilliant blob.

I feel that I do understand the general message: once I have encountered the Phoenix, the Journey will have a lot left to go, but I can have no settled expectations as to what will occur. The Ancestor is being very careful not to feed that tendency of mine, my addiction to the illusion of control. Oh, and Fox would be a good companion.

Afterward, it occurred to me what the scary passage had represented. The Ancestors were telling me that they were pissed off at how I'd dissed them yesterday.

63. September 20, 2022

> "Trance can be described as the deconstruction of ordinary perception as well as the habitus of quotidian interactional patterns and customary organization of time, all in order to empower the subject to experience the accustomed life-world in a more vital manner."[28]

I asked Fox to accompany me to the Lower World to meet the Phoenix. While not explicitly requesting Badger to join us, I did, on an impulse, in the midst of thanking my other Spirit Helpers, sing the song he'd given me. Where did that impulse come from?

Badger and Fox meet me in the Garden. I think, Badger being so closely tied to self-image may not be the best choice to assist in seeking dismemberment. But I don't dismiss him.

It's as dark as a heavily overcast night.

We wander around for a while, enter a clearing. I have a side view of the nearby porch of the House of Childhood, a black trapezoid. I see the House several times, from different angles. Why am I circling it? Do the rats have anything to do with it?

Straining at the increasing darkness, I realize that I am trying to see what I want to see. I relax.

Branches overhead stand out a bit more distinctly against the now-grey sky. I ask Badger and Fox to show me to the Lower World. They say we're on our way there. My sense of motion sharpens. I am in the tunnel. There's

28 Jonathan Garb, *Shamanic Trance in Modern Kabbalah* (University of Chicago Press 2011), p. 22

a place where the rock walls glow red. Then, I'm in the Ancestors' cavern, but they are not present.

I am beyond the Ancestors' cavern. I see signs that I am in or approaching the Lower World: glimpses of dark waters, the familiar ridge lines gliding by, jagged against a steel bright sky. I see them as if from above, and at the same time they move past as if I am below them.

I call the Phoenix to please meet me. Nothing new happens for a while, then there's a large, glaring eye, a raptor's beak, talons. They each appear several times, and each time there's a frisson of emotion, hard to identify. "Who are you?"

"I am the Phoenix."

"Please take me to my dismemberment," I ask, but nothing happens. I ask, "What can you do for me?"

"I will tear you and eat you."

Suddenly, all I'm seeing is shifting, formless blobs of light and color. An intricate, sharply defined, metallic image explodes into view and quickly is gone. I wonder if it is the golden door the Ancestors told me about, but it has disappeared before I can be sure. I don't think to ask. I become aware that the Phoenix is eating my liver. There's no pain, but I have a hollow feeling below my belly.[29] *Several times, I feel my body tense. Several times, I become aware that I need to remember to breathe.*

There follows a long period during which the predominant color stabilizes as a pale, pinkish lavender, reminiscent of the crown chakra. Overhead I see what looks similar to the pebbled overcast that is my Guardian Spirit

29 A friend to whom I read the notes of this Journey pointed out that the liver is located above the belly, not below it. On the other hand, the liver is on the right side of the abdominal cavity, as was the area that I felt hollowed out. Maybe the Phoenix was working its way up the right side of my body.

in certain moods, but I feel that I am not looking at a sky or anything celestial. Rather, I am in a widened portion of a tubular space bounded by the uneven surface of a lavender membrane. Inside the Phoenix? The possibility suggests itself. I am not sure. A voice tells me I am in the Phoenix's stomach. This moves me closer to certainty, but doubt persists. What is the provenance of that voice? Is it me, or a Spirit talking? I suspend judgment. I think, if I am in the Phoenix's stomach, then it is going to poop me out. I do seem to move sluggishly through the pinkish-lavender organ. But the Journey ends before I exit.

64.

I was feeling rather more spacey than I had felt after my previous several Journeys. The spaciness continued for hours, even increasing while I wrote my notes and thought after thought, memory after memory rushed into consciousness.

At first, I wallowed in uncertainty as to what if anything had occurred. Something that may be important, to be sure, but what? Returning from a Journey was like waking up from a dream. I had to pull it back from the depths it already had more than halfway disappeared into. My handwriting bordered on the illegible as I hurriedly jotted down bits and pieces as fast as I could bring them to the surface.

Reviewing my notes, it was clear what had happened: just exactly what seemed to have happened. I had gone to the Lower World, met the Phoenix, and the Phoenix ate me after politely telling me that it was going to do so. Lights out. Presumably, being dismembered, I had died some sort of dreamworld death. Then the lights had come back on, in the Phoenix's digestive tract.

So. . . what should be the next step? I had been theorizing that my initial uncertainty about the Journey was just another of ego's myriad defenses against ceding control of consciousness to the dreamworld. I toyed with the idea of returning to the Garden, finding ego in Spirit form, and demanding angrily that it should get out of my way. Or maybe ego would be found in the Lower World. Either way, though, why take such a confrontative not to say combative approach against this loyal and generally capable servant?

Looking in another direction, maybe Fox and Badger had led me at first to the House of Childhood for a reason. So much of my work in the dreamworld thus far had related to that traumatic time in my earliest youth, during the first stages of ego development, when my mother had been temporarily lost to me. Perhaps ego should not be seen as an overbearing, over-reaching, manipulative, paranoid tyrant, who needed to be slapped down. Perhaps, instead, ego reacted to stress as a frightened, lonely toddler, in need of comfort and protection. In that case, it was fairly clear what I should do next.

I had been introduced to the trope of the "inner child" during psychotherapy. Although my therapist and I incorrectly had aligned my "recovered memory" of violation with then-current theories of child sexual abuse, that perspective hadn't been entirely mistaken. It had led to a reasonably effective therapeutic intervention. After all, there had been real trauma, whatever its precise cause may have been. Once I had recognized the bewildered, damaged little boy whom I carried within, I had assumed a protective, nurturing stance toward him.

I now believed that the dreamworld had shown me that the therapy most likely had been based on a distorted view of the facts, which had limited its effectiveness. I had been like a well-meaning stranger who blunders helpfully into a wounded child's life, earning some degree of trust for good intentions, but also distrusted because of his obvious cluelessness. Now that I more accurately understood the wounded child's situation, I needed to revisit him in trance, to finish the job.

> **Email Message, September 20, 2022, 4:15 p.m., re: Dismemberment:** Wendy, just a short note to tell you that you retain the distinction of being the only person you know who was eaten by rats. Unless I'm profoundly misinterpreting my last Journey, the Phoenix ate me. Oddly, the Journey ended with me still inside the Phoenix's digestive tract. I was waiting for the Phoenix to poop me out, but it didn't. I'm not sure what that means. Maybe we'll talk about that next time we meet?

> **Email Message, September 20, 2022, 6:46 p.m.:** Something to be proud of, I guess!
> The first thought that came to me when reading your note was that you've said you like to take things slowly . . . for that reason, perhaps you've connected with a Phoenix who has intestinal motility issues?

It's tempting to end this section on such note, because Wendy's email so perfectly captured my feeling of light-hearted relief at the time. There, that wasn't so bad, was it? But I would be untrue to something important, to stop here. In the event, the high degree of trepidation with which I'd tiptoed up to my meeting with the Phoenix may have been misplaced. On the other hand, it derived from a sense of what is at play in the dreamworld. As to what I felt that is, and how serious the stakes may be, I do not think that I can express it better than I did in Canto XXX of *Once Was Lost*:

It's the patch behind my house.
There in the corner's the scraggly arborvitae
overshadowed by buckthorn saplings.
Lying near it, a thing the length of my forearm, a
grey streak on the creeping charlie.
Stepping cautiously closer, I see it's a rabbit.
Why is it lying there, so still?
Then I see it's breathing, and I see the
straight, clean slash that opens its
belly front to back, revealing a jumble of
lilac, lavender, brown, and yellow
organs, still tightly packed and glistening.
Did a hawk do this, then drop you?
As I bend a little closer, you scrabble
with your stiff front legs, dragging your
shoulders to interpose your head between
me and your body, fixing on me an
eye's expressionless, dark blue bead.
I retreat to the shed for a spade to
end this misery, but, when I return, the
rabbit's dead. I bury it.
Hanging the spade back on its peg, I'm followed
by your dark blue bead
and the strength that utterly spent itself on
facing whatever I might bring you.
Gyres in darkness a bead as blue as the ocean
I face in my shock and awe.

65. September 22, 2022

I thanked the Ancestors and my Spirit Helpers, and asked the latter to meet me by the big pine near the House of Childhood to accompany me to the Lower World to visit the House of Emotion and to seek the wounded child there. I asked Mama Bear to bring along the cubs, thinking her maternal protectiveness might be appealing if the search were successful, and the cubs might be good playmates. "We have some caregiving to do," I said, and wondered if I were setting too many goals for this Journey.

Once again, the Garden is dusky. And I'm viewing it sideways—the trees growing horizontal, left to right. I look around for the big pine tree, then realize I am trying to make things happen. Just take the trip, I remind myself. Now the trees are vertical and stand out a bit more clearly.

A crimson glimmer: Fox. Fox says, "You can't do it by yourself." Badger's black eye and striped mask. Earlier, I saw vague shapes in the woods that I thought might be the cubs. Scotoma-like sparkles seem to represent Sky. We're all here. Fox pops into view ahead, a hair of fire leading me down into the earth. I follow.

We are moving rapidly through a tunnel. We enter the cave of the Ancestors. I ask if they are present. Yes, they are. I ask for their blessing on this Journey. They say, "You have it." I ask if there's anything I can do for them. They say, "Just take the trip."

Surprisingly quickly, the ridgelines begin to appear that indicate I am in or approaching the Lower World. I call to Phoenix to come to me and take me to the Emotion

House. A shiny, black, curved, eagle-like beak fills my gaze. Although my point of view is in front of the beak as if it were facing me, I feel that I might be wearing it.

We begin to move through the corrugated landscape and misty waters of the Lower World. Literally "through," although I try to gain altitude to fly above them. Unlike the earlier Journey in which I rode on a Cardinal's back above my Garden, clinging to its feathers, the bird's body visible to me, I do not see the Phoenix. No head, no shoulders, no wings, nothing.

The golden door flashes before me. I head straight into it. Then I am rising up the inside of a golden tower. When I reach the top, no grand vistas open before me. Instead, it's treetops in the mist, seen from above. The tower is very tall.

I resume flying. Now I am going higher and higher, into the cloud cover. The mist is a light brownish tan. I fly through it for a long time. I ask the Phoenix to find the House of Emotion, but there's no response, just continued flight through the featureless, tannish mist. That's when I consciously accept that I have become the Phoenix.

I ask my Spirit Helpers how to find the House of Emotion. They don't respond, at first. Then, far ahead, somewhat down and to the left, there's a muffled flare, like lightning seen through clouds. "That way," I say. I head in that direction.

Suddenly, there are saturated colors. In the middle of a sheet of pure black, a blood-red door. I have reached the House of Emotion.

Within, it is vivid and chaotic. Throughout my visit here, I see in swift, infrequent flashes the treetops that seem to be ubiquitous in my Lower and Middle Worlds. What they're doing in the House of Emotion, I have no idea.

A majestic, gem-like swirl, like a fluid stained-glass window, identifies itself as Anger. A grey-brown skull hiding within pulsing blobs is Fear. I can't describe the multitudinous images Confusion presents me with, except for the final, perhaps emblematic one of a mushroom-shaped cloud that drains away downwards into nothingness. Remembering the Ancestors' advice, I face each of them. I ask each of them to help me find the wounded child. None of them replies.

But . . . I later cannot remember exactly when . . . there is a vivid glimpse of a pair of human eyes hiding in a bright place. The lozenge of brightness in which the eyes appear—a photographically realistic pair of eyes, set between the little I can discern of a similarly realistic forehead and cheeks—is yellow, the elongated diamond shape of a gap in a venetian window shade when someone has pushed apart two slats a bit to peek through. It blinks out before I can react.

66. September 27, 2022

Why had I been greeted in the House of Emotion by Fear, Anger, and Confusion, and not any of the many other feelings, mostly positive, that I knew were in my repertoire? It seemed obvious to me that these were the wounded child's emotions, that is, my emotions during the time that my mother was withdrawn from me. Since I had visited the House of Emotions in order to find the wounded child, those emotions had met me at the door.

This morning, while I was meditating, that train of thought moved several stops further. I had experienced great difficulty during the infancies of both my children, so much so that I had gone into psychotherapy not many months after the birth of the eldest for fear that I might become abusive. Fear, anger, and confusion had dominated my emotional life during this period. The therapy had helped me to limp through without fulfilling my apprehensions, but it was not until either of my children had passed the age of three that I had begun to take pleasure in parenting. Before that, in each case it had been a terrible trial. I never had felt that I truly understood why. What dawned on me this morning during meditation was that the responsibility of caring for my infant children, with their helplessness, vulnerability, and demands, had touched down to my own, formative trauma, reviving the emotional triumvirate that had ruled my toddlerhood.

After meditation, I prepared to Journey. I smudged my room, donned my choker, and blew the shofar. I thanked my Helper Spirits by name for all that they had given me. I hesitated, and included Phoenix with the other four. I called on them to "meet me by the big pine . . . in the case of Phoenix, if that is appropriate," and to join and support me on this Journey to the Lower World "to visit the House of Emotion and to heal and recover the wounded child." A rush of tenderness and love surprised me as I said this last, close to tears and with a whispering voice that was all the more expressive for its sudden loss of power. I laid down in my bed, put in my earbuds, and commenced the drumming. I covered my eyes.

I approach the Garden through the veil. It takes a long time to break through, and even then, I'm seeing everything as if through gauze. I look for the big pine. Maybe I see it, maybe I don't. I look for my Helpers. Maybe they join me, maybe they don't. The Garden disappears.

Maybe I'm in a tunnel, maybe not.

The quality of the blackness changes to that of the

Ancestors' cavern, but they're not there. It takes unusually long to pass through it. There are lots of bright colors and geometric, symmetrical designs, but none of them means anything to me.

Maybe I'm entering the Lower World, and maybe I'm not. I see no sign of the Phoenix. Maybe I have become the Phoenix, I think hopefully. I caw a couple of times. It sounds louder than I expected.

Maybe I'm flying through the Lower World, and maybe I'm not.

I sense Spirits around me, but they won't talk. I can't find the golden door.

Maybe I'm in the House of Emotion, maybe not.

There's an Owl. I ask what it can do for me. It says, very faintly, it can show me where the wounded child is. I ask what I can do for it. The Owl says, "You are my master." Having no idea what this could mean, I guess that the Owl sees me as the Phoenix. A Phoenix could rule other birds, perhaps. I ask the Owl to take me to the wounded child. I worry mildly that the child will be scared of the Phoenix. I follow the Owl, flying seemingly at random above the clouds, until the Journey ends.

No Journey is a failure. The Spirits also had shown me nothing on several earlier Journeys, but they always had meant something by it. There was the Journey to the Reflecting Pool, in which Sky had me stare at his mostly unchanging reflection in the water for almost the entire time. I'd interpreted that as Sky's way of saying that the action I was contemplating would have no substantial effect. More recently, the Ancestors had set the channel to the dreamworld equivalent of static to show me the value of expectations. This time, I speculated, perhaps I had already accomplished the Journey's purpose with my epiphany during meditation and in the emotions that had climaxed my preparation ritual. There was nowhere left to go and nothing left to do. The child, discovered in hiding on the previous Journey, had been welcomed home. I felt pretty good about it.

67.

Fox says, now your eyes are closed,
what if what you see,
the colors, shapes, hints of faces

swirling, blending, and flying apart,
that you like to imagine are merely
prelude to sleep, instead have meaning:

what if you're as clueless as you'd be
watching a telenovela that stars
octopi; they're all speaking ancient

wordless Ursprache, uncaptioned.
Though you've half a dozen fewer
brains, you spoke it once, too,

but—you remember?—you forgot.
Every morning day and night
your whole life flashes

green coded streams descending
behind your eyes, and you don't
recognize a thing.

68. October 18, 2022

The workbook had a few more places to send me before I'd have completed the section on Healing. One of them was the "Healing Lagoon" in the Middle World, where I should note the color of the water, "take a dip," and leave an offering.

> *The Spirit Helpers appear in rapid sequence against a background of dusky forest: Fox, Badger, Mama Bear, Father Sky. Plus, some others not previously recognized as such: an Owl, a raptor that might be Phoenix.*
>
> *We move swiftly through the forest. Time seems compressed. I see the moon overhead and realize that it's the middle of the night and we have been traveling for hours. Then daylight spatters through the dense overhead foliage.*
>
> *I look down at water, sapphire blue and amethyst purple. Then up at the arboreal canopy. Then down at the water. Then up at the trees. Like a glitchy DVD, this view of alternating water and trees continues for a long time. There's a transitional period of blobby kaleidoscopery, then vision slowly stabilizes.*
>
> *I'm surrounded by water. Standing in it, wading, diving, swimming. Somebody else is here, I'm not sure who. I catch some hints of Fox and splash him. He doesn't splash back. For a fraction of a second, I see a flash of gold, the golden door, the golden tower, beyond which is the Lower World's House of Emotion. I play in the water some more.*
>
> *A human face sinks into the Lagoon. I focus on the nose, the nostrils, the open mouth. It is the Wounded Child, surprised and drowning in the healing waters.*

"Drowning" in these waters is a good thing. The Child and I swim around for a while.

I have dived especially deep and long, skimming the uneven, rocky bottom, a long time down there. Holding my breath indefinitely does not seem to be a problem as I float just above the submerged, dark, conical hillocks.

Suddenly, it's as if I am standing on a reef or sandbar, getting a very quick glimpse across at least half a mile of open water to what might be a low, wooded island. Palms in front of a bank of deciduous trees under a bright blue sky peppered with a few small, fluffy, white clouds. The water reflects the robin's egg sky. It's an oddly tropical scene, a postcard photo, clear and sharp.

I don't see the Child anymore, but I know he's here.

Now I'm swimming again in the Lagoon instead of looking across it. The water has taken on a purplish/lavender tinge that reminds me of the crown chakra and Neshama. I begin to smile. Quiet pleasure perfuses my body. It lasts the remainder of the Journey.

The Child and I walk along the shore of the Lagoon, a low-lying coast like one sees in Maine or Nova Scotia, smooth, grey, water-rounded stones among large, dark, angular rocks and boulders. Surf's up, white water swirling among and over the rocks. We wade into a calm tidal pool, looking for shells, small fish, crabs, and such. We don't catch any, but numerous small, unidentifiable creatures, red as cooked lobsters, stir near our feet. The Child is having fun.

The drum signals that it's time to come home. I tell the Lagoon I am leaving it my book—this book—as an offering, and heave the manuscript in its binder out over the now-flat waters. An ocean sprite leaps through the surface, arms outstretched, and catches it.

69. November 6, 2022

I returned to the House of Emotion, to observe what might have changed.

The Garden always seems dark these days, at first when I arrive. I have invoked the assistance and support of my Spirit Helpers for this Journey, but I'm a bit surprised when the one who greets me most warmly in the Garden is Owl. A few other animals show their faces, but too fleetingly to recognize them with confidence. Was that Fox? But it was grey-brown, not red. And who were those beings with big, round, buggy eyes astride a proboscis? Well . . .

I ask Owl to show me to the Lower World. I also ask Owl, "What can I do for you?" I remember, or perhaps Owl reminds me, that of late I haven't been keeping my promise to Sky to burn incense. That's been in connection with a disruption in my meditation practice due to a bad case of piriformis syndrome making it difficult to sit. Apparently, I think, the smudge with which I prepare for Journeys isn't enough. Owl says, "You are my master." I wonder if this means I have become Phoenix already, even though we are not yet in the Lower World.

We are following a tunnel. Dim, blue light barely outlines the rocks that bulge in its roughly circular walls. We reach the Ancestors' cavern. They're here, flying hither and yon in the blackness, wearing their scary masks, which this time look like the masks Balinese ritual dancers wear, fierce and cartoonishly demonic.

I ask, "Why do I always pass through you on my way to the Emotional House?"

The answer comes from one of them or perhaps from them collectively, "Who gave you your emotions?"

I ask, "Please show me the way out of your cave to the Lower World."

Almost immediately, the sign appears, the jagged tree line, the steely sky.

Now I briefly see Phoenix, head and beak as if viewed from her shoulders. Am I riding, this time? I don't see Phoenix again. We fly along. From kaleidoscopic blobularity evolves an evenly overcast sky, blue-purple. We fly beneath the clouds. I wonder why I am looking up at them, not down at whatever we're flying over. Why don't I fly through the clouds, to be above them?

Where are the golden tower and the golden door? The knowledge comes, without being told, they are straight ahead. I keep on thinking I glimpse them through the clouds, the veil thinning from time to time until tantalizingly something behind it shows almost nakedly, but they never definitely come into view.

After a long flight, abruptly we pass through the clouds into another place. There is no door or gate to mark the transition. I recognize it as inside the House of Emotion, but at the same time a voice says, "no." I think, that voice probably was mine, reacting in my nit-picky way to the changed mode of arrival, and I can disregard it.

Spirits are here. None of them appears to be Anger, Fear, or Confusion. I watch them flow about, somewhat like oil slicks, somewhat like fish in an aquarium. One has something like a head (for a little while; none of them holds a solid form; this "head" lasts unusually long before it melts into something else), a big square with a jagged bottom edge, like a side view of one of those hammer-shaped meat tenderizers, a cube with pyramidal studs on the business face. I say, "Who are you?" It answers, "Love." Love as a meat tenderizer!

Another Spirit takes center stage. Unlike the others that have eddied across my field of vision, it persists there. It is a swirling, purplish thing. It has a face, but the face keeps metamorphosing into other faces: human, animal, the Phoenix. It looks rather like the Mozilla Firefox internet browser icon, a mammalian ouroboros, if that were a moving image and if it kept shifting hues and shape like light in water. I think and am told more or less simultaneously that I am looking at the roots of Neshama.

It took me a little longer than usual to return to normal awareness of my body and its physical situation. I felt spacier than usual. These things seemed to fit the pattern of a brush with Neshama.

I went for a walk. It was an unseasonably warm day—sandals in November! During the first few minutes outside, I experienced an unusual perceptual phenomenon.

Normally, while strolling along, my eyes move from this thing to that thing, their focus roving from object to object. A loud motorcycle will draw my attention, or a man on a ladder painting a building, or a gnarly tree branch, or a beautiful jogger. I imagine this is the way it is for everyone who's not staring at a screen or lost in interiority, listening to headphones. A walk along a busy street is a series of individual, narrow, random impressions that flit in and out of consciousness, chasing each other mostly beyond the reach of memory.

But not long into my walk along this busy, four-lane throughfare, I noticed that I unintentionally was doing something different. My gaze held steadily on what was before me. That in itself was not very odd, of course; the unusual thing was that no part of the oval optical was privileged. My gaze held steadily on what was before me, that is, not on a particular person or thing, but on everything all at once, everything in my entire field of vision, from edge to edge, side to side and top to bottom. Nothing was singled out as a center of attention. Moreover, it was not an unfocused stare; rather, everything in sight was as sharp and well defined as if I were focused on it alone. There's a term in photography for a picture in which the foreground and the background appear equally sharp, no softening or blurring of the one or the other. Such a picture is said to have depth of field. That was the case with me. The buildings across the street to my left, the cars passing beside me and approaching me from a distance, the buildings all along my side of the street, the person in a black jacket about a hundred yards ahead of me walking in the same direction, all were equally well-defined.

It was not mere sensation. It is hard to describe, this sense of watching everything all at once in the moving scene through which one is moving, of feeling no special, individual relationship to anything in the known vicinity but of existing rather as a point of perspective moving through innumerable other points of perspective, individual existences all interconnected just by virtue of being here, me among them neutral as to each and neutrally part of it all. I had approached a similar level of conscious, unvalenced omnisentience a very few times in meditation, but never one so complete and effortlessly sustained.

After about five minutes, my perception shrank to normal. I made several attempts to regain that state of holistic awareness, fixing my eyes steadily ahead and resisting the impulse to focus on any one thing, but every time I felt the effort and couldn't get there.

70. November 12, 2022

The workbook's last exercise is to hold a party in one's Garden, a sort of graduation ceremony. I felt it marked my readiness to move on to first grade. Reading what masters like Corine Sombrun, Hank Wesselman, and Wendy Halley[30] have written about their explorations, I get an inkling how far I have yet to go.

I blast my horn in every direction!
There! Did you hear that?
The room smells sweetly of sage.
You all are invited—

each and every one of you!
known and unknown
who has helped in
what we have done
what we are doing
what we will do—

Fox Badger Mama Bear and Bear Cubs
Father Sky Cardinal
Owl Phoenix—Rats? well, maybe—
Angel Ancestors Grandma
Mom and Dad Neshama
Vic and whoever—

30 *See* Wendy S. Halley, *Slaying the Mouse: A True Story of Healing in the Spiritual Realms* (self-published 2012). For that rarest of things, an indigenous shaman's book-length exposition in his own telling, see Davi Kopenawa and Bruce Albert, *The Falling Sky* (Harvard University Press 2013).

to a Garden party
in the clearing near the
House of Childhood
(from its porch
refreshments may be served)

honoring and celebrating
US
for
what we have done
what we are doing
what we will do.

Yes! The trees whisk the sky
in a circle around us.
Here, first to arrive,
the smoothly groomed,
grinning Fox, its eyes
yellow today and gleaming.
Badger's striped snout.
The Ancestors arrive in a bunch
like tourists off a bus and
for a while everything is
them taking selfies.

The place is getting crowded.
It's unclear to me
what's going on.

I do what I always do at parties.
Not mingling.
Watching the laughing heads

thrown back, the talking heads
thrust forward. A busty woman
in a brown, one-piece swimsuit
(who is she?)
walks by, not looking my way.

There's a talon. Hello, Phoenix.
Haven't seen Mama Bear
Maybe she couldn't get a sitter.

Spirits keep on coming over,
telling me about great deals
on flights to the Lower World.
(Why? I'm confused. Maybe
I have had too much to drink?
Maybe the trance is trying
to send me down there,
away from here.)
I brush them off.

Sky keeps trying to show me something.
I wish someone would use their words.

Sunlight lances through the green foliage
and brown columns where Owl and I
hang out a while together,
the way I do at parties,
escaping from the crowd
into an individual.
I couldn't tell you
what we talk about,
if anything. Maybe
we perch quietly.

I make a speech.
I thank them all
several times in various ways.
I offer them festive chocolates.

Where is the House of Childhood?
Sure it's nearby, I can't find it,
until I do.
I wander through dark interiors.
I don't remember this
tall, skinny cupola,
dark against a bright background,
its outline wavery as if
reflected in rippling water.

Timeless breathlessness:
Neshama's appearance,
however long all too brief,

leads to a ribbon snaking
around rocks among the trees,
a stream feeding into—yes!
hurray! we're all going for a
dip in the Healing Lagoon!

But the driving drum
stutters to a stop and
I fall behind, miss the swim
gliding homeward

back the way I came.
Not yet all the way

I pause in my seat to
gaze at the now-deserted stage,
its high proscenium arch
empty of all but blackness and the
blue and purple retinal ghosts
of extinguished floods.

ACKNOWLEDGMENTS

My early education in shamanic trance was guided throughout by Wendy Halley's workbook, although I skipped some of the exercises, did some of them out of order, and not infrequently digressed from the lesson plan.

I thank Samara Anderson for ushering me to the schoolhouse door, and Wendy Halley for her perceptive, caring, gentle, patient, Montessori-style guidance once I stepped inside.

During the writing of this book, my dear friends Deborah Gaynor, Stephen Pilcher, Wendy Sue Harper, and Robin Hoppe and I met weekly to play Wingspan, a wonderful board game built on avian themes. (Sadly, it lacks a Phoenix.) The four of them listened eagerly to each Journey the week after its description rolled off the word processor. Their delight and interest in my adventures helped sustain mine through the not infrequent periods of discouragement and confusion that beset me along the way.

I am gifted with wonderful friends, including my two teachers, Samara Anderson and Wendy Halley, who joined Jennifer Spackman, Stephen Kottler, Maura Murphy, and my sister Lise Kennedy to slog through the book's first draft with good humor, good will, and surprisingly unanimous advice as to what needed to happen before the bird in this cage could sing.

Another gift has been my editor at Green Writers Press, Ferne Johansson, who has the literary equivalents of a sculptor's eye, a musician's ear, an engineer's understanding of how things work, and a diplomat's tongue, all adorning a person I have found it a pleasure to work with.

ABOUT THE AUTHOR

Born in 1952, Seth Steinzor grew up in the suburbs of Buffalo, New York. His parents encouraged his verbally precocious creativity. After graduating from Middlebury College in 1974, a job with the local Public Defender led Steinzor to law school. He slept on his 1979 Juris Doctor degree until 1990 when Vermont Attorney General Amestoy promoted him from Civil Rights Investigator to Assistant Attorney General. During the next twenty-seven years, he represented the State, married, fathered two children, divorced, and wrote most of *In Dante's Wake*. He retired in 2017 to a life of woodworking, gardening, voracious reading, and writing.